# KATY BESKOW

# Vegan FAKE-OUT

PLANT-BASED
TAKE-OUT CLASSICS
FOR THE ULTIMATE
NIGHT IN

Photography by Luke Albert

Hardie Grant

QUADRILLE

# INTRODUCTION

We all love food delivered straight to our door. It's one of life's little pleasures, and a great way to try delicacies from around the world, in the comfort of our own homes. Ordering a take-out means you don't have to cook from scratch, and you can relax with friends and family while someone else does the cooking. So why don't we all order one every night of the week?

Firstly, take-out food is costly. Convenience never comes cheap, especially when the food is prepared and cooked elsewhere and often driven directly to you. Not only are you paying for the ingredients, chefs and transportation costs, you're paying for packaging, which is likely to be made up of non-recyclable single-use materials. Even though vegan menu options are becoming increasingly available on restaurant menus, it can often be difficult to feel reassured that there are suitable cross-contamination methods in place, or to be sure that an animal product hasn't been accidentally used in the dish.

I'm not saying that you should never order in, but before you do, think about the cost savings, reduction in waste, health benefits, reassurance in what you're cooking and satisfaction you will have when you rustle up your favourite restaurant classic, in your own kitchen.

In this book, you'll find 70 recipes for your favourite weekend treats across five chapters: American, Italian, Indian, Chinese and Middle Eastern. Whether it's just for you, or you're cooking for family and friends, there's something in here for everyone. You'll find recipes that take just 15 or 30 minutes to cook, slow cooker recipes that do the hard work for you, and handy one-pot dishes.

All of the ingredients used in these recipes are readily available from supermarkets, making it easy for you to get started. I've simplified dishes without compromising on taste, and used healthier cooking methods where possible, so you can enjoy tasty food without the fuss. You won't even need any specialist kitchen equipment. Challenge yourself to make the dishes faster than your local restaurant could deliver!

I hope you enjoy your time in the kitchen, using these plant-based recipes to create fresher, vegan-friendly versions of your Friday-night favourites. Pour yourself a glass of wine or a cup of tea, pull together the ingredients and have fun cooking up these take-out classics, which are kinder on your purse, better for the environment, kinder to animals, and better for you.

Eating in is the new eating out!

# WHY TAKE-OUT
# WHEN YOU CAN FAKE-OUT?

**Before you reach for that menu, consider all of the benefits
of making your own restaurant classics, at home.**

## 1

### SAVE TIME

Ordering in may seem like the quicker option, but by the time you decide what to eat, order online or on the phone, then wait for the restaurant to make and deliver your food, it's likely you'll be able to cook something within that time. Some of the recipes in this book use just one cooking pot, so you'll spend even less time washing up! If time really is of the essence, then why not try making some fifteen-minute dishes, such as Butter chickpeas (page 87), Speedy satay stir-fry (page 117), Fettuccine alfredo (page 64) or Mango and lime lassi (page 96).

## 2

### SAVE MONEY

Convenience never comes cheap, and that certainly applies to the convenience of having dinner cooked and delivered to your door. Cooking your favourite restaurant classics at home is remarkably cheaper, using store cupboard ingredients and readily available fresh ingredients. Save the money that you would have spent on your usual order safely in a money box, then treat yourself to that special something you've always wanted. Need some cheap eats inspiration? Try the Tear-and-share dough balls (page 51) and Red wine ragù with tagliatelle (page 57).

## 3

### TRUST THE INGREDIENTS

So, you've read the menu and can't see any animal ingredients; you hope it's vegan-friendly, but how do you ever really know if your dishes have been made without cross-contamination in the kitchen, or if a non-vegan ingredient has accidentally been added? Creating your own versions at home means that you can choose the ingredients yourself, and add what you're happy with. With peace of mind that your dinner is 100 per cent vegan, it will taste even better without any worries about consuming animal products. For an unexpected vegan treat, cook up Jackfruit doner kebabs (page 149) with Date, nutmeg and orange pastries (page 153) to finish.

# 4

## CONTROL THE FAT, SALT AND SUGAR

No newsflash required – we know that fast food establishments can pack their dishes with huge amounts of fat, salt and sugar, most of which is unnecessary. By cooking your favourite dishes at home, you can control how much you put into your food. When used appropriately and in moderation, these ingredients will take your food from simple to sublime. For healthier alternatives to the classics, try Singapore noodles (page 114), Carrot and cashew Chinese curry (page 118) and White chocolate mousse and kiwi (page 127).

# 5

## LESS PACKAGING

Think about how your last delivery was packaged: polystyrene boxes, plastic sauce pots, non-recyclable linings inside cardboard – all brought to you in a flimsy plastic carrier bag. Take-out food is often packaged in single-use plastics and even any cardboard packaging is difficult for waste agencies to recycle due to grease staining. By cooking at home, you're cutting out the need for these materials, which are destined for landfill. Do think about recycling or reusing containers and packaging that your store cupboard essentials are purchased in, and where you can, opt for fresh ingredients that have minimal or no packaging. Enjoy these low waste recipes: Spicy sweet potato baked fries (page 33) and Black bean sloppy joes (page 36).

# FAKE IT 'TIL
# YOU MAKE IT

**Follow these tips to get the most from your weekend treat, without the need to order in!**

**One of the best things about having food delivered is that the it arrives hot, with no effort required.**
In each chapter of this book, I've included a slow cooker recipe, so you can prepare the ingredients earlier in the day, and let the slow cooker do all of the hard work while you get on with better things. Then you can come home to a delicious, hot meal without having to fork out for take-out! Many of the recipes in this book are suitable for freezing, meaning you can batch cook and freeze them in heatproof containers, then simply defrost and reheat when needed. Freeze in individual portions, in sealable containers, not forgetting to label them with what they are and the date you made them. It's also useful to write these frozen portions into your weekly meal plan, then you won't forget about them sitting in the freezer.

**Always wanted to try something new without the risk of paying restaurant prices for a dish you won't like?**
Creating the dish at home is a great way to give it a try, and you can modify it for your personal taste too. It's easy to get stuck in a rut when ordering in, so use this as an opportunity to experience something new. It may well become your new signature dish!

**There's nothing like gathering your friends and family around for a meal.**
Imagine how impressed they'll be to discover that you cooked all of the food! Think about preparing some of the dishes in advance, to save time and effort when your friends turn up, or stick to recipes with quicker cooking times. Even more fun – get friends and family involved in the cooking process! As you've made savings by making the dishes at home, you could even treat your guests to a homemade dessert.

**Indulge in your regular junk food rituals, whether it's enjoying a cold beer, bingeing on Netflix, or eating in your pyjamas!**
One of the perks of not eating out is that you can create the rules. Make it fun!

**If ordering in gives you a sense of treating yourself, begin to think of simple cooking as treating yourself.**
The process of cooking can be very mindful, so enjoy it! It's both reassuring and satisfying to produce dishes of your own for you and friends to enjoy.

# HANDY STORE CUPBOARD INGREDIENTS

Having a small stock of essential ingredients available means that you can whip up home-cooked restaurant classics, whenever you fancy it.

## CHOPPED TOMATOES, PASSATA AND TOMATO PURÉE

Canned chopped tomatoes make an excellent base for many dishes, from soups to burritos. They are cheap to buy, easy to store, and have a long shelf life. Passata is chopped tomatoes that have been sieved, creating a smooth and rich sauce, perfect for pasta and dips. When cooking with chopped tomatoes or passata, taste the dish as you cook it, as tomatoes can be quite acidic – a simple pinch of sugar will take any harsh acidity away. Tomato purée (paste) is thicker and has a concentrated flavour – use to top pizza or add a burst of flavour to curries.

## COCONUT MILK

Coconut milk is a versatile ingredient, perfect to add creaminess to curries, soups and desserts, without the need for dairy products. Choose full-fat canned varieties for the silkiest texture and a rich flavour.

## JACKFRUIT

Canned or vacuum-packed jackfruit is now available in most large supermarkets, and is easy to prepare by simply draining away the water or brine, rinsing with water, and either 'pulling' the chunks apart or leaving them whole. Use in place of meat, or processed meat alternatives, for doner kebabs, curries or pulled and stuffed into pittas.

## BEANS AND PULSES

Keep a stock of canned chickpeas, butterbeans, red kidney beans and green lentils, for meals in minutes that give you versatility as well as a cost-effective source of protein. Simply drain away the water from the can, and rinse thoroughly to remove any unwanted 'canned' flavour. Dried red lentils are cheap and long-lasting, perfect to make a flavourful dhal, or for bulking out any slow-cooked dish.

## PASTA AND NOODLES

Most dried pasta in the supermarket is egg-free, as it is simply made of durum wheat, but always check the label before purchasing. Dried pasta is easy to store, and cooks in under 10 minutes for a fast dinner. When choosing noodles, avoid those found in the chilled section of supermarkets, as they are likely to contain eggs. Instead, look for rice noodles or ready-to-wok varieties in the ambient section, and always read the label to ensure they contain no animal ingredients.

## SPICE BLENDS AND PASTES

In addition to a selection of your favourite spices, mixed spice blends have been created by experts to contain a variety of flavours, such as curry powder, garam masala and Chinese five-spice. This means that you can have perfectly crafted spices taking up less room in your cupboard, with minimal fuss when cooking. Pre-blended curry pastes (again check that they are vegan) make an excellent base; simply keep refrigerated once opened for fuss-free flavouring.

## OILS

Sunflower oil is an excellent oil for cooking with, as it has no overpowering taste and is versatile for roasting, frying and baking. Save extra-virgin olive oil for dressing salads and pasta, as it has a stronger, greener flavour, and is a more expensive option.

## SUGAR AND SALT

One benefit of cooking your own take-out-style dishes is that you can control the amount of sugar and salt that is in your food. When used in moderation, sugar reduces acidity in tomato-based dishes, and provides the perfect sweetness in desserts and baked goods. Salt enhances the flavour of a finished dish; use moderately and choose good-quality sea salt flakes for a purer flavour.

# FRESH FAVOURITES

Take your home cooking to new levels with fresh
ingredients that are just right for the job.

## TOFU

Blocks of extra-firm tofu require draining
of moisture before use. To do this, press
using a tofu press. Alternatively, wrap in
kitchen paper or a clean kitchen towel
and lay on a plate. Place another plate on
top of the block, then add heavy-based
pans or a few books as a weight to press
and remove excess liquid. Press for 1 hour.
Use extra-firm tofu for firmer pieces that
you can cut, fry or bake. Silken tofu is
sold in semi-liquid form and is best used
in desserts and sauces that require a
creamy base.

## DAIRY-FREE MILK, CHEESE AND YOGURT

There is a growing selection of alternatives
to dairy available in supermarkets.
Ultra-high temperature treated (UHT)
plant-based milks (soya, almond, oat
etc.) last for longer in the cupboard,
and only need to be refrigerated once
opened. Unsweetened soya milk is the
most obvious one to use in cooking, but
try a few plant-based milks to find your
favourite. Vegan cheeses are now readily
available from most supermarkets. Choose
from your favourite hard cheeses or cream
cheeses to suit the recipe. Unsweetened
soya or coconut yogurt are also great to
have to hand, for their versatility to use in
both savoury and sweet dishes.

## FRUIT AND VEGETABLES

Whether you buy fruit and vegetables
from large supermarkets, local markets,
or collect from an allotment, be sure
to choose those that look vibrant, fresh
and appetizing. For the best flavour and
most cost-effective way of eating, choose
produce that is in season, where possible.
Having a selection of frozen vegetables
in your freezer ensures you can enjoy the
ingredient out of season, with minimal
waste as you only use what you need
before the bag goes back into the freezer.
Vegetables that cook well from frozen
include butternut squash, peas, sweetcorn,
sweet potato and spinach. Don't forget
to add unwaxed lemons and limes to your
shopping list (waxed citrus fruit are coated
with an animal ingredient so aren't vegan),
as a squeeze of the vibrant juices can really
lift a dish, with minimal effort.

## FRESH HERBS

Alongside a few dried herbs, have some
fresh herbs available to transform your
dishes with bursts of fresh flavour. Woody
herbs such as rosemary, sage and thyme
work well when dried, however leafy
varieties such as flat-leaf parsley, coriander
(cilantro), basil and mint are best used
fresh and added to a dish just before
serving. Store them in a light, cool place,
with stems in a glass of water for longevity.

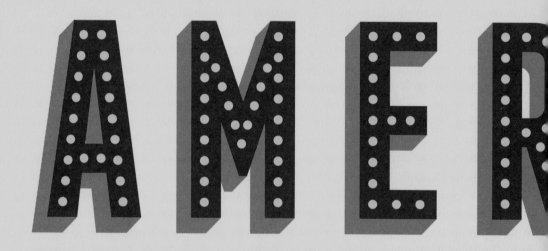

## MENU FOR 4

Finger-lickin' wings, creamy bowls of mac 'n' cheese, tacos and, of course, blueberry muffins; could American-style junk food be any better? And when it's all vegan, easy to prepare and delicious to eat, it's always a good time to indulge in an all-American night in.

# STICKY BBQ CAULIFLOWER WINGS WITH RANCH DIP

## SERVES 4 AS A SIDE DISH OR SNACK

Finger-lickin' snacks don't come more delicious than these sticky cauliflower wings, with their crunchy, golden crust. Pimp up shop-bought BBQ sauce with chilli flakes for heat that is moreish and satisfying. Panko breadcrumbs give a perfectly crisp coating, and can be found in most large supermarkets or Asian supermarkets. Serve straight from the oven, with a cooling ranch dip.

**For the cauliflower wings**
200ml (generous ¾ cup)
　 BBQ sauce (ensure vegan)
2 tbsp sunflower oil
2 tsp garlic powder
½ tsp dried chilli flakes
100g (2 cups) panko breadcrumbs
1 medium cauliflower, broken into bite-
　 sized florets with some stem remaining
1 spring onion (scallion), thinly sliced

**For the ranch dip**
4 tbsp chilled vegan mayonnaise
2 tbsp chilled unsweetened soya yogurt
generous handful of chives, finely chopped
small handful of flat-leaf parsley, finely
　 chopped
generous pinch of sea salt and black pepper
pinch of smoked paprika
extra-virgin olive oil, for drizzling

✳

Preheat the oven to 200°C/400°F/gas mark 6 and line two baking trays with baking parchment.

In a bowl, mix together the BBQ sauce, oil, garlic powder and chilli flakes.

Arrange the panko breadcrumbs on a plate. Dip a cauliflower floret into the BBQ sauce mix, shake off any excess, then roll in the panko breadcrumbs. Place on a lined baking tray and repeat until each floret is coated.

Bake in the oven for 15 minutes, remove from the oven and carefully use a spatula to turn the florets before returning to the oven for 10–15 minutes until the breadcrumbs are evenly golden.

Meanwhile, make the ranch dip. Mix together the mayonnaise and soya yogurt then stir in the chopped chives and parsley. Season to taste with sea salt, plenty of black pepper and finish with a pinch of paprika and a drizzle of olive oil.

Remove the sticky BBQ wings from the oven, scatter with the spring onion and serve hot, with the cooling dip.

 **GET AHEAD**
Make extra spicy BBQ sauce and keep it covered in the fridge for up to a month for quick and easy fake-outs.

# DIRTY NACHOS

## SERVES 4

*These hot, loaded tortilla chips are perfect for sharing as an appetizer, or as a cheeky snack. Melted vegan cheese, green chillies, tangy gherkins and meaty little slices of sundried tomatoes top freshly baked tortilla chips; serve with chive mayonnaise for a cooling dip.*

4 large soft white tortilla wraps, sliced
   into triangles
2 tbsp sunflower oil
pinch of garlic powder
100g (3½oz) medium-strength vegan
   cheese, grated
1 green chilli, thinly sliced into rounds
6 sundried tomatoes in oil, drained and
   roughly chopped
2 small pickled gherkins, sliced into rounds
handful of chives, finely chopped
2 tbsp chilled vegan mayonnaise
pinch of sea salt and black pepper
extra-virgin olive oil, for drizzling
pinch of smoked paprika

Preheat the oven to 180°C/350°F/
gas mark 4.

Arrange the tortilla triangles in a large,
deep baking tray and drizzle over the
sunflower oil. Rub the oil over the triangles
evenly. Sprinkle with garlic powder, then
bake for 5 minutes until just crisp.

Carefully remove the baking tray from the
oven and sprinkle over the grated cheese,
chilli, sundried tomatoes and gherkins.
Return the tray to the oven and cook for
a further 3–4 minutes until the cheese
begins to melt.

Meanwhile, mix together the chives and
mayonnaise in a small bowl, reserving a few
chives for serving. Season to taste with sea
salt and black pepper, then finish with a
drizzle of olive oil.

Remove the tortilla chips from the oven
and transfer to a large serving plate along
with the chive mayonnaise. Dust over a
pinch of smoked paprika, scatter over the
reserved chives and serve.

### ✦ GET AHEAD
The toppings can be prepared up
to 3 days in advance, then kept in
airtight containers in the fridge.

# ULTIMATE MAC 'N' CHEESE

## SERVES 2 GENEROUSLY

**Look no further for the ultimate comforting mac 'n' cheese (that also happens to be vegan), ready in just over 30 minutes. Team with Pecan and cranberry slaw (opposite) or Dirty nachos (page 21) for an all-American experience!**

**Sauce suitable for freezing**

2 medium sweet potatoes, peeled and evenly chopped into 2cm (¾in) chunks
200ml (generous ¾ cup) unsweetened soya milk
150g (5oz) medium-strength vegan cheese, grated
handful of chives, finely chopped
generous pinch of sea salt and black pepper
200g (7oz) dried macaroni (ensure egg-free)

✳

Preheat the oven to 200°C/400°F/ gas mark 6.

Bring a large pan of water to the boil over a high heat, then add the sweet potatoes. Boil for 15–20 minutes until the potato chunks are tender.

Use a slotted spoon to remove the sweet potato from the pan (reserving the water to cook the macaroni) and place them in a high-powered jug blender. Pour in the soya milk and blitz on high speed to create a smooth sauce. If you don't have a high-powered jug blender, put the cooked sweet potato and milk into a large bowl and use a stick blender to blitz until smooth.

Stir most of the grated vegan cheese and chives into the sauce, then season to taste with salt and pepper.

Pour the macaroni into the pan of boiling water and simmer over a medium-high heat for 8–10 minutes until al dente. Drain thoroughly and return to the pan.

Pour over the sauce and stir through to combine. Transfer to a baking dish, scatter over the remaining grated vegan cheese and chives and bake in the oven for 10 minutes until bubbling. Divide between bowls and serve.

 **GET AHEAD**
The sauce can be made up to 2 days in advance; simply allow to cool and store in an airtight container in the fridge. The sauce can also be frozen.

# PECAN AND
# CRANBERRY SLAW

## SERVES 4

Throw together this creamy, tangy slaw that combines two of America's classic
flavours: pecan and cranberry. Serve with Roasting tray fajitas (page 32),
Ultimate mac 'n' cheese (opposite) or enjoy as a side dish with Breaded
cheese dippers (page 39).

1 small white cabbage, thinly sliced
1 carrot, peeled and grated
2 spring onions (scallions), finely chopped
8 pecans, roughly chopped
2 tbsp dried cranberries
2 rounded tbsp vegan mayonnaise
pinch of black pepper

In a large bowl, mix together the cabbage,
carrot, spring onions, pecans and dried
cranberries.

Spoon in the mayonnaise and stir to coat
all of the vegetables.

Season with black pepper just before
serving.

**GET AHEAD**
This slaw will keep for 2 days in an
airtight container in the fridge.

# DEEP PAN TORTILLA PIZZA BITES

## MAKES 8

Friday-night food doesn't get any better than this! These crisp, deep-filled mini pizzas are the perfect size to nibble on while you do the more important things in life, like binge-watching Netflix. What's more, they take just 10 minutes to cook, ideal for when you need that pizza fix quickly.

**Tortillas suitable for freezing**

2 tsp sunflower oil
3 large soft tortilla wraps
6 tbsp tomato purée (paste)
150g (5oz) medium-strength vegan
   cheese, grated
small handful of frozen or canned
   sweetcorn (no need to defrost if using
   frozen; it will cook in the oven)
pinch of dried oregano
8 button mushrooms, halved
8 cherry tomatoes, halved
fresh black pepper

✳

Preheat the oven to 180°C/350°F/gas mark 4. Use a pastry brush to grease 8 cups of a deep muffin tray with sunflower oil, then set aside.

Lay out the tortilla wraps on a flat surface. Use a scone cutter (large enough to fill the muffin tin cup) to press out 16 circles.

Press one single tortilla round into each oiled muffin cup, then brush the surface with a little oil. Press on another tortilla round to make a double layer.

In a mixing bowl, stir together the tomato purée, vegan cheese, sweetcorn and oregano, then spoon the mix evenly into the tortilla cups.

Share the mushrooms and tomatoes evenly between each tortilla cup, pressing them down slightly, then bake in the oven for 10 minutes until the edges are golden and the filling is bubbling.

Allow to cool for a couple of minutes, then use a teaspoon to lift the pizzas from the tray and arrange on a serving plate. Grind over a little black pepper.

**GET AHEAD**
The tortilla rounds can be made in advance and kept in an airtight container for 2–3 days. They can even be frozen and defrosted before use, for fuss-free preparation.

# EASIEST-EVER BURRITOS

## SERVES 4

Whether you enjoy a loaded burrito in the evening, or as a hearty breakfast or weekend brunch, throw the ingredients into your slow cooker and let it do all of the hard work, for a Tex-Mex classic that is fuss-free and full of flavour. Delicious served with Pecan and cranberry slaw (page 23).

**Filling suitable for freezing**

2 sweet potatoes, peeled and evenly chopped into 2cm (¾in) chunks
1 onion, roughly sliced
1 red (bell) pepper, roughly sliced
1 x 200g (7oz) can sweetcorn, drained
1 x 400g (14oz) can chopped tomatoes
1 x 400g (14oz) can red kidney beans, drained and rinsed
2 tsp mild chilli powder
1 tsp smoked paprika
¼ tsp ground cinnamon
4 tbsp basmati rice
generous pinch of smoked sea salt
handful of coriander (cilantro), roughly chopped
4 large soft tortilla wraps
100g (3½oz) medium-strength vegan cheese, grated

✳

Preheat the slow cooker by setting it to low.

Put the sweet potato, onion, red pepper, sweetcorn, chopped tomatoes, kidney beans, chilli powder, smoked paprika and ground cinnamon into the slow cooker.

Stir in the rice with 100ml (scant ½ cup) cold water, then place the lid on the slow cooker. Cook on low for 6 hours until the sweet potato has softened and the rice is cooked. Season to taste with smoked sea salt, then stir in the coriander.

Lay out each tortilla wrap on a separate piece of foil, then sprinkle over the grated vegan cheese. Spoon in the slow-cooked filling and tightly wrap the tortillas with the foil around them. Serve hot.

### TAKE-OUT TIP
Don't be tempted to add any more liquid to the slow cooker during cooking, as the liquid does not evaporate unlike on the hob. You want the filling to be a little starchy for the perfect burrito, which is why basmati rice is my preferred choice for this recipe.

### GET AHEAD
The slow-cooked filling is suitable for freezing; alternatively keep covered in the fridge for up to 2 days.

# THE REUBEN BAGEL

## SERVES 4

The Reuben is the ultimate American sandwich, traditionally made with very non-vegan pastrami and cheese, with pickles and a mustard dressing. Create an alternative to vegan pastrami using glazed aubergine (eggplant) pan-fried to be crisp on the outside and meaty in the centre. Load with vegan cream cheese, sauerkraut and a feisty Russian dressing. Meat-eaters love this sandwich too (I won't tell them it's vegan if you don't).

sunflower oil, for frying
2 tbsp light soy sauce
¼ tsp smoked paprika
1 aubergine (eggplant), sliced into 1cm (½in)
   thick rounds

**For the Russian dressing**
2 tbsp chilled vegan mayonnaise
1 tsp English mustard
1 tsp tomato ketchup
small handful of dill, finely chopped
pinch of sea salt

**For the bagels**
4 plain bagels, sliced in half
4 heaped tsp vegan cream cheese
small bunch of dill
4 tbsp sauerkraut

✳

Add a glug of oil to a large frying pan (skillet), then place over a medium heat while you prepare the aubergine.

In a bowl, whisk together the soy sauce and smoked paprika. Dip the aubergine slices into the soy sauce mix until both sides are coated.

Use tongs to add the aubergine to the pan, then increase the heat to medium-high.

Cook the slices for 5 minutes on each side. The outer skin should be crisp, and the centre golden brown. You may have to cook the aubergine slices in batches; simply keep the cooked slices warm between kitchen paper while you cook the remainder.

In the meantime, prepare the Russian dressing. In a bowl, mix together the mayonnaise, mustard, ketchup, dill and salt, then set aside.

When all of the aubergine slices are cooked, place the sliced bagels face down in the pan and lightly toast for 1–2 minutes. Once toasted, spread each bagel base with vegan cream cheese. Add two slices of aubergine, some sprigs of dill and a spoonful of sauerkraut. Top with the Russian dressing and finish with the lid of the bagel. Serve hot.

**GET AHEAD**
The aubergine and Russian dressing can be prepared a day in advance and kept refrigerated in an airtight container.

# COLA SWEET POTATO TACOS WITH SWEETCORN SALSA

**SERVES 4**

Sticky cola-glazed sweet potatoes and red beans make the perfect taco filling, especially when it's brightened with a tangy and fresh salsa. You can char the sweetcorn under the grill, or use a blow torch if you have one, to add smokiness to the salsa. A family favourite that everyone will love.

**Filling suitable for freezing**

1 tbsp sunflower oil
2 medium sweet potatoes, peeled and
    cut into even 1cm (½in) dice
½ tsp ground cinnamon
½ tsp dried chilli flakes
300ml (1¼ cups) cola
1 tbsp BBQ sauce (ensure vegan)
1 x 400g (14oz) can red kidney beans,
    thoroughly drained and rinsed
small handful of coriander (cilantro),
    roughly torn
generous pinch of smoked sea salt
8 crunchy taco shells, to serve

**For the sweetcorn salsa**

1 x 200g (7oz) can sweetcorn,
    thoroughly drained and rinsed
1 small red onion, finely diced
juice of ½ unwaxed lime

✳

Heat the oil in a large pan, add the sweet potatoes and cook over a medium-high heat for 5 minutes until they begin to soften slightly. Stir through the cinnamon and chilli flakes.

Pour in the cola and BBQ sauce, then simmer for 15–20 minutes until the cola has reduced and become sticky. Stir through the kidney beans until coated in the sticky sauce. Sprinkle in the coriander and season to taste with smoked sea salt.

To make the sweetcorn salsa, stir together the sweetcorn and red onion. Squeeze over the lime juice.

Spoon the cola sweet potatoes and beans into the taco shells and top with the sweetcorn salsa. Serve immediately.

 **GET AHEAD**
The cooked cola sweet potatoes and beans can be frozen, then thoroughly defrosted and reheated before enjoying. The salsa is best served fresh.

# ROASTING TRAY FAJITAS

## SERVES 4

Some nights, you just want to throw a few ingredients into a roasting tray and
let the oven do all of the hard work. Gently roast (bell) peppers, mushrooms
and red onion with Mexican-inspired spices, with minimal effort from you.

1 red (bell) pepper, roughly sliced
1 yellow (bell) pepper, roughly sliced
2 red onions, thinly sliced
2 Portobello mushrooms, brushed clean
   and roughly sliced
2 tbsp sunflower oil
2 tsp fajita seasoning
1 tsp smoked paprika
generous pinch of smoked sea salt
   and black pepper
small handful of coriander (cilantro)
   leaves, torn
juice of ½ unwaxed lime
4 large soft tortilla wraps
1 avocado, peeled, stoned and sliced
1 baby gem lettuce, quartered and
   core discarded

✳

Preheat the oven to 200°C/400°F/
gas mark 6.

Arrange the peppers, red onions and
mushrooms in a deep roasting tray.

In a small bowl, mix together the oil, fajita
seasoning and smoked paprika, then drizzle
over the vegetables, turning them to
ensure they are all coated in the spiced oil.
Roast in the oven for 25 minutes.

Carefully remove the roasting tray from
the oven and season with smoked sea
salt and black pepper. Scatter over the
coriander and stir through the lime juice.

Lay out the tortilla wraps and fill each
one with avocado slices and baby gem
lettuce leaves. Liberally spoon in the
roasted vegetable filling and fold the
wraps up into fajitas.

 **TAKE-OUT TIP**
✳  Fajita seasoning is a pre-mixed spice
   blend, found in the spice section
◦  at the supermarket. It saves you
   the time and effort of mixing the
   individual herbs and spices!

# SPICY SWEET POTATO BAKED FRIES

## SERVES 2

**Who doesn't love sweet potato fries? This batch is baked instead of deep-fried; just make sure that your oven is preheated before baking to give you fries that are crisp on the outside and fluffy on the inside. Coat with the spice mix for a true take-out taste.**

2 medium sweet potatoes, peeled and sliced into 1cm (½in) thick fries
2 tbsp sunflower oil
1 tsp smoked paprika
1 tsp garlic powder
1 tsp sea salt
pinch of ground cinnamon

✳

Preheat the oven to 220°C/425°F/gas mark 7.

In a large bowl combine the sweet potato fries and sunflower oil.

In a smaller bowl, mix together the smoked paprika, garlic powder, sea salt and cinnamon. Toss this through the sweet potato until all the fries are evenly coated.

Spread out evenly over two baking trays, making sure that none of the fries are overlapping – this will ensure that they cook evenly and become crisp. Bake in the oven for 20 minutes until golden brown and crisp at the edges. Serve hot.

✦ **GET AHEAD**

The spice mix can be mixed and stored in an airtight jar for up to 4 weeks – why not use it to spice up jacket potatoes? This recipe is easy to double-up if you're serving more than two people.

# BLACK BEAN SLOPPY JOES

### SERVES 4

**If you're looking for inexpensive fast food, this will become your go-to dish! While a vegan burger in a toasted bread bun is a popular choice, sloppy joes are traditionally American, fun and messy to eat, which all of the family will love!**

1 tbsp sunflower oil
2 red (bell) peppers, finely diced
6 spring onions (scallions), roughly chopped
2 tsp soft brown sugar
2 tsp smoked paprika
pinch of ground cinnamon
2 x 400g (14oz) can black beans, thoroughly drained and rinsed
4 tbsp tomato purée (paste)
4 tbsp BBQ sauce (ensure vegan)
4 bread buns, split
generous pinch of smoked sea salt
1 avocado, peeled, stoned and sliced
small bunch of rocket

✳

Heat the oil in a pan, add the red pepper and spring onions and cook over a medium-high heat for 2–3 minutes until the pepper begins to soften. Stir in the brown sugar, smoked paprika and cinnamon and cook for a further minute.

Pour in the black beans, tomato purée and BBQ sauce and simmer for 10 minutes, stirring frequently to avoid sticking.

In the meantime, gently grill or toast the bread buns until lightly toasted.

Season the black bean mix with smoked sea salt to taste, then spoon generously into the bread buns. Top with slices of avocado and rocket and serve immediately.

 **TAKE-OUT TIP**
Canned black beans can be found in large supermarkets, and are time-saving as well as being easy to use. Canned green lentils or aduki beans make great alternatives if you don't have black beans available.

# BREADED CHEESE DIPPERS

## SERVES 2 GENEROUSLY

**Crisp on the outside, with hot, oozing cheese on the inside, vegan cheese dippers are decadent yet so simple to make. Cheese sticks are usually deep-fried, but this simple version is baked. The trick is to toast the breadcrumbs in a pan before baking, to speed up the cooking process and avoid any melting mess on your baking tray! Serve with a small bowl of tomato ketchup, for dipping.**

5 tbsp panko breadcrumbs
generous pinch of black pepper
200g (7oz) block of vegan cheese
 (Cheddar or mozzarella-style), chilled
2 heaped tbsp vegan cream cheese

✻

Preheat the oven to 200°C/400°F/gas mark 6.

Spoon the breadcrumbs into a large frying pan (skillet) and toast over a medium-high heat for 3–5 minutes until lightly golden, shaking the pan occasionally to avoid burning.

Season the breadcrumbs with black pepper, then tip into a shallow bowl and allow to cool a little.

Carefully slice the block of cheese in half, then cut each half into 5 thick sticks. Spread the cream cheese over all surfaces of each cheese stick, then dip into the breadcrumb mix, pressing them firmly on.

Arrange the breaded cheese sticks on a baking tray and cook for 5–7 minutes until the cheese is hot. Carefully remove from the oven and serve immediately.

 **TAKE-OUT TIP**
Panko breadcrumbs give an extra crunchy bite to these cheese dippers. You'll find them in large supermarkets, often near the Japanese ingredients.

# BEER-BATTERED TOFISH AND CHIPS

## SERVES 4

Cruelty-free doesn't have to mean flavour-free, with a golden beer batter encasing tender tofu. It's thanks to nori seaweed sheets that the tofish has a flavour of the ocean (you'll find nori in the world food aisle of large supermarkets).

**For the chips**
4 large King Edward potatoes, peeled and cut into 2cm (¾in) thick chips
2 tbsp sunflower oil
sprinkle of malt vinegar
pinch of sea salt

**For the beer-battered tofish**
200g (generous 1½ cups) plain (all-purpose) flour
2 tbsp cornflour (cornstarch)
pinch of ground turmeric
small handful of fresh dill, finely chopped
1 tsp sea salt
generous pinch of black pepper
300ml (1¼ cups) cold beer (ensure vegan)
2 x 280g (9½oz) blocks of extra-firm tofu, drained and pressed (see page 14)
4 sheets of sushi nori
500ml (generous 2 cups) sunflower oil
unwaxed lemon wedges, to serve

✳

To make the chips, preheat the oven to 200°C/400°F/gas mark 6. Rinse the chipped potatoes under cold water, drain and pat dry. Lay the chips on a baking sheet in an even layer. Drizzle with the sunflower oil, then bake for 50 minutes until golden and crisp.

Meanwhile, make the beer batter. Stir together the flour, cornflour, turmeric, dill, sea salt and black pepper in a large bowl. Slowly pour in the beer and whisk to get rid of any lumps. Rest the batter in the fridge while you prepare the tofu.

Slice each block of pressed tofu horizontally, so you have 4 thin rectangles. Press a sheet of nori over one side of each tofu slice. Heat the sunflower oil in a large, deep frying pan (skillet) over a medium heat. Dip the tofu slices in the batter to coat fully then use a slotted spoon to place them in the pan for 3–4 minutes, before turning and cooking the other side until light golden in colour.

Remove the chips from the oven and sprinkle with vinegar and salt. Serve the tofish and chips hot, with wedges of lemon.

 **TAKE-OUT TIP**
Tofu requires draining and pressing to give it a firmer texture. See page 14 for detailed instructions on how to do this.

# BLUEBERRY MUFFIN IN A MUG

## SERVES 1

Avoid leaving the house when you need a sweet fix by creating this
coffee-shop favourite in your own kitchen, using store cupboard ingredients.
Enjoy warm with a freshly brewed Americano.

4 tbsp self-raising flour
2 tbsp granulated sugar
pinch of ground cinnamon
10 fresh blueberries, sliced in half
4 tbsp sweetened soya milk
1 tbsp sunflower oil
1 tsp good-quality vanilla extract

✳

In a large, microwave-proof mug, mix
together the flour, sugar and cinnamon.
Stir through the blueberries.

Spoon in the soya milk, oil and vanilla
extract and mix to create a thick batter,
ensuring any dry mixture at the bottom
gets combined.

Place the mug in an 800W microwave and
cook for 1 minute 30 seconds. Carefully
remove from the microwave and allow to
stand for 1 minute before enjoying.

 **TAKE-OUT TIP**
Roughly slicing the blueberries in half
will allow them to become oozy, sweet
✳   and gooey. If you don't have the time
or inclination to slice the blueberries,
simply squish them to release the
juices before stirring into the mix.

# NO-BAKE
# LIME PIES

## SERVES 4

Key lime pie is an American classic; however it can be hard to source key limes in the UK. Key limes have a sweeter flavour than standard limes, but the humble citrus fruit is still delicious, particularly when combined with maple syrup and vanilla. You will notice an unexpected ingredient in the list – spinach leaves – which add a gorgeous green hue to the dessert without reaching for that bottle of green food colouring (you won't taste the spinach, I promise!).

2 tbsp vegan butter
6 ginger biscuits (ensure vegan), broken into a fine crumb or blitzed in a food processor
350g (12oz) silken tofu
finely grated zest and juice of 2 unwaxed limes
3 tbsp maple syrup
1 tsp good-quality vanilla extract
small handful of spinach leaves

✳

Melt the vegan butter in a pan over a low heat, stirring occasionally. Once the butter has melted, add the ginger biscuit crumbs and stir until coated.

Press the biscuit mixture into the bases of 4 ramekin dishes and flatten with a spoon.

Place the silken tofu, half of the lime zest, the lime juice, maple syrup, vanilla extract and spinach leaves in a food processor or high-powered jug blender. Blitz until completely smooth and silky.

Spoon the lime mixture liberally into the ramekins on top of the biscuit base. Scatter with the remaining lime zest.

Chill the pies in the fridge for at least 4 hours until set.

 **GET AHEAD**
These pies require some chilling time.
✳  Four hours will allow them to set,
○  but feel free to make them a day in advance and keep refrigerated until served.

## MENU FOR 2
**Rosemary salt polenta chips** (page 61)
**Sicilian-style antipasti pizzas** (page 60)

## MENU FOR 4
**Classic lasagne** (page 50)
**Tear-and-share dough balls** (page 51)

Pizza, pasta and no-meat balls – oh my! Italy has gifted us countless tasty treats, ones that should never be reserved just for the weekend. Gather family, friends or just yourself for Italian take-out classics that suit every occasion (and are so simple to cook up!)

# TOMATO BRUSCHETTA

## SERVES 4 AS A SIDE DISH OR STARTER

**Pour yourself an aperitif and plate up some fresh and delicious bruschetta. The perfect way to start a meal, Italian style.**

1 small white baguette (French stick), cut into 2cm (¾in) diagonal slices
generous drizzle of extra virgin olive oil

**For the tomato topping**
300g (10oz) mixed baby tomatoes, roughly quartered
generous drizzle of extra virgin olive oil
small handful of basil leaves, roughly torn
generous pinch of sea salt and black pepper

✳

Place a griddle (grill) pan over a medium-high heat. Drizzle the bread slices with olive oil then carefully place the slices on the hot griddle pan. Griddle for 3–4 minutes on each side until even grill lines appear on the bread.

Meanwhile, mix the tomatoes, olive oil and basil in a bowl. Season to taste with sea salt and black pepper.

Use tongs to carefully remove the toasted bread from the griddle pan and place on serving plates. Spoon over the tomato topping.

 **GET AHEAD**
✳ The tomato topping can be made
∘ a day in advance and stored in the
fridge in an airtight container. Bring
the tomatoes to room temperature
before loading over the toasted bread
for the most authentic flavour.

# CREAMY GARLIC MUSHROOMS WITH CIABATTA

### SERVES 2 AS A SIDE DISH OR STARTER

Luxurious, simple and delicious – here button mushrooms are sautéed with garlic, thyme and vegan cream. Serve with toasted ciabatta drizzled with extra virgin olive oil, for unashamed dipping down to the last drop.

1 tbsp sunflower oil
200g (7oz) button mushrooms, brushed clean, large ones halved
3 garlic cloves, crushed
1 sprig of fresh thyme
150ml (generous ½ cup) single soya cream
2 thick slices of ciabatta
generous pinch of sea salt and black pepper
small handful of flat-leaf parsley, finely chopped
1 tbsp extra virgin olive oil

✳

Heat the oil in a large frying pan (skillet), add the mushrooms and cook over a medium heat for 5–6 minutes, stirring frequently, until browned and fragrant.

Add the garlic and thyme and cook for a further minute.

Stir through the soya cream and allow to simmer for 3–4 minutes while you toast the ciabatta in a toaster or under the grill (broiler) until lightly golden.

Remove the thyme sprig from the pan and discard. Season to taste with sea salt and plenty of black pepper and scatter over the parsley.

Drizzle the olive oil over the toasted ciabatta and serve with the creamy mushrooms spooned over.

**TAKE-OUT TIP**
For a quick main meal, stir the creamy garlic mushrooms through cooked egg-free pasta.

# CLASSIC LASAGNE

## SERVES 4 GENEROUSLY

Imagine coming home to a perfectly cooked lasagne, with just
10 minutes of hands-on work. Sounds too good to be true? Let your
slow cooker put in all of the effort to create this delicious lasagne that
will feed a family. Serve with green salad and a slice of crusty bread.

**Suitable for freezing**

1 tbsp sunflower oil
1 onion, diced
2 celery sticks, finely diced
2 carrots, peeled and finely diced
1 garlic clove, crushed
1 tsp dried oregano
1 tsp dried mixed herbs
generous glug of red wine (ensure vegan)
1 x 400g (14oz) can chopped tomatoes
1 x 400g (14oz) can green lentils, drained
   and thoroughly rinsed
8 dried lasagne sheets (ensure egg-free)
4 tbsp soya cream
100g (3½oz) medium-strength vegan
   cheese, grated
sea salt and black pepper

✳

Heat the oil in a large pan, add the
onion, celery and carrots and cook over a
medium-high heat for 2–3 minutes until
the onion begins to soften. Add the garlic,
oregano, mixed herbs and wine then cook
for a further minute.

Pour in the chopped tomatoes and green
lentils, then stir to combine. Remove from
the heat and season with salt and pepper.

In the slow cooker pot, lay in a lasagne
sheet followed by a layer of the herby lentil
mix. Repeat this layering process until all
of the lasagne sheets are used, finishing
with a final layer of the herby lentil mix.
Cover with the lid and set the slow cooker
to 'low'. Slow-cook for 6 hours.

Remove the lid from the slow cooker
and spoon over the cream. Sprinkle with
vegan cheese then place the lid back on for
10 minutes until the cheese begins to melt.
Serve hot.

 **GET AHEAD**
✳   Make this in advance, allow to cool
◦   and then freeze in individual portions.
    Reheat thoroughly in a microwave or
    oven before enjoying.

# TEAR-AND-SHARE DOUGH BALLS

## SERVES 4 AS A SIDE DISH OR STARTER

Everyone loves a warm dough ball (or two), served with lashings of garlic butter for that all-important dipping. This tear-and-share version is simple to make with store cupboard ingredients, and is set to be a real crowd-pleaser!

**Suitable for freezing**

300g (2½ cups) strong white bread flour, plus extra for dusting
½ tsp fast-action dried yeast
generous pinch of sea salt
2 tbsp sunflower oil, plus extra for greasing

**For the garlic butter**
100g (3½oz) vegan butter
3 tbsp extra virgin olive oil
3 garlic cloves, crushed
small handful of flat-leaf parsley, finely chopped
generous pinch of sea salt

✳

Place the flour, yeast and salt in a large bowl (ensuring the yeast and salt are placed on opposite sides of the bowl). Stir in the sunflower oil, along with 200ml (generous ¾ cup) lukewarm water, and bring together to form a dough.

Sprinkle a clean work surface with a little flour, then tip the dough out and knead for 10 minutes until soft and elastic.

Lightly grease a baking dish with oil. Divide the dough into about 12 even pieces and roll them into balls. Arrange in the baking dish, positioned close to each other but not touching (they will increase in size during proving). Cover the baking dish with cling film (plastic wrap), then place the dish in a warm place to prove for 45 minutes.

Meanwhile, prepare the garlic butter. Mix together the vegan butter, olive oil, garlic and parsley in a small bowl, then season to taste with sea salt.

Preheat the oven to 200°C/400°F/gas mark 6. Remove the cling film from the baking dish, then bake the proved dough balls in the oven for 15–20 minutes until golden. Remove from the oven and immediately brush with some of the garlic butter. Serve warm with the remaining garlic butter on the side for dipping.

✦ **GET AHEAD**

The dough balls are suitable for freezing once cooked: simply defrost thoroughly and reheat before serving. Whip up the garlic butter fresh to get the best flavours from that all-important dip.

# BAKED
# GNOCCHI CAPRESE

## SERVES 2 GENEROUSLY

Love ordering in because it means you have less washing up to do? Try this one-pot, prepare-and-bake gnocchi caprese – all the flavours and colours of Italy, without loads of cleaning up!

**Suitable for freezing**

1 tbsp sunflower oil
2 garlic cloves, crushed
500g (1lb 2oz) passata
generous handful of fresh basil, finely chopped (reserve a few small leaves to garnish)
1 tsp sugar
6 sundried tomatoes in oil, drained and halved
500g (1lb 2oz) potato gnocchi (ensure egg-free)
6 tsp vegan cream cheese, chilled
generous pinch of sea salt and black pepper

✳

Preheat the oven to 200°C/400°F/ gas mark 6.

In a lidded hob-to-oven dish, add the oil and garlic and cook over a low-medium heat for 2 minutes until the garlic has softened.

Pour in the passata, chopped basil and sugar, then stir to combine.

Remove from the heat and stir in the sundried tomatoes and gnocchi. Place the lid on the dish, then bake in the oven for 30–35 minutes until the gnocchi has become tender.

Remove the dish from the oven and take off the lid. Spoon in the cream cheese in teaspoon-sized amounts, pressing them gently into the sauce. Scatter over the reserved basil leaves and season with sea salt and black pepper.

 **TAKE-OUT TIP**
Keep a packet of potato gnocchi in the store cupboard (or fridge), for fuss-free dinners. You'll find it vacuum-packed in most supermarkets, but do check to make sure it is egg-free.

# MAGIC PIZZA BASES

## MAKES 1 LARGE PIZZA OR 2 INDIVIDUAL SIZED PIZZAS

**With no yeast, proving or kneading, you can whip up the perfect thin and crispy pizza more quickly than the delivery driver can bring one! With this recipe, you'll wonder why you've never made your own pizza from scratch before. If you prefer a thicker base, try my Sicilian-style antipasti pizzas (page 60).**

2 tbsp extra virgin olive oil, plus extra
  for greasing
200g (generous 1½ cups) plain
  (all-purpose) flour, plus extra for dusting
½ tsp fine sea salt
½ tsp dried oregano

✳

Preheat the oven to 200°C/400°F/gas mark 6 and lightly oil a round pizza baking tray (or lightly grease a regular baking sheet if you are making two smaller pizzas).

Add the flour to a large bowl and mix in the sea salt and oregano.

Make a small well in the centre of the flour mix, then pour in the extra virgin olive oil, along with 100ml (scant ½ cup) lukewarm water. Combine using a spoon, then use your hands to bring the mixture together

into a smooth, even dough. The dough should be stretchy and smooth.

Turn out the dough onto a lightly floured surface, then use a rolling pin to roll the pizza base to a thickness of 2mm (¹⁄₁₆in) as one large or two individual pizzas.

Place the pizza base or bases on the oiled baking tray, then cover with your favourite sauce and toppings. Bake in the oven for 15–18 minutes until the edges are golden and crisp.

✦　**GET AHEAD**

Chop your favourite pizza toppings, including mushrooms, (bell) pepper, cherry tomatoes and grated vegan cheese, a day in advance, then keep chilled in sealed containers.

# RED WINE RAGÙ WITH TAGLIATELLE

## SERVES 4

The rich and herby flavours of Italian cooking are not exclusive to your favourite Italian restaurant; with a few store cupboard ingredients you can create a tasty ragù in the comfort of your own home. Most dried pasta available in the supermarket is egg-free, as it is simply made from durum wheat semolina, but do check the ingredients before purchasing.

**Ragù suitable for freezing**

1 tbsp sunflower oil
1 onion, diced
1 carrot, peeled and diced
4 closed-cup mushrooms, brushed clean and diced
2 garlic cloves, crushed
1 tsp dried oregano
1 tsp dried mixed herbs
generous glug of red wine (ensure vegan)
1 x 400g (14oz) can chopped tomatoes
pinch of sugar
1 x 400g (14oz) can green lentils, thoroughly drained and rinsed
4 sundried tomatoes in oil, drained and roughly chopped
300g (10oz) dried tagliatelle (ensure egg-free)
4 tbsp extra virgin olive oil
generous pinch of sea salt and black pepper
handful of small basil leaves, to garnish

✳

Heat the oil in a large pan, add the onion, carrot and mushrooms and cook over a medium-high heat for 3–4 minutes, stirring, until the carrot begins to soften.

Add the garlic, oregano and mixed herbs and stir through for 1 minute. Pour in the red wine and reduce down for 2–3 minutes.

Stir in the chopped tomatoes, sugar, lentils and sundried tomatoes, then simmer for 15–20 minutes, stirring occasionally to prevent burning, until some of the liquid has evaporated.

Meanwhile, cook the tagliatelle in a large pan of salted boiling water for 8–10 minutes until al dente. Drain, then drizzle through the olive oil.

Spoon the ragù through the pasta and use tongs to ensure it is easily distributed. Season to taste with sea salt and black pepper, share between warmed bowls and scatter over the basil.

**GET AHEAD**
The ragù can be made up to 3 days in advance and kept in the fridge in a sealed container, and is also suitable for freezing. Tagliatelle is best cooked fresh, as the texture is affected during chilling and freezing.

# NO-MEAT BALLS WITH MARINARA SAUCE

## SERVES 4

There's nothing more comforting than no-meat balls and a classic marinara sauce.
Serve with egg-free spaghetti (100g/3½oz per person) cooked until al dente,
or loaded into sub rolls for the ultimate hot sandwich.

**Marinara sauce suitable for freezing**

**For the no-meat balls**
3 tbsp sunflower oil
1 medium (about 300g/10oz) aubergine
 (eggplant), evenly diced
1 red onion, roughly chopped
1 tsp dried oregano
4 thick slices of white bread
generous pinch of sea salt and black pepper
handful of flat-leaf parsley, finely chopped

**For the marinara sauce**
1 tbsp sunflower oil
2 garlic cloves, crushed
1 x 400g (14oz) can chopped tomatoes
1 tsp sugar
handful of flat-leaf parsley, finely chopped

✳

Heat 1 tablespoon of oil in a large frying pan
(skillet) and add the aubergine, onion and
oregano. Cook over a medium-high heat
for 10–12 minutes, stirring occasionally,
until gently browned. Blitz the bread in a
food processor to fine breadcrumbs. Spoon
the breadcrumbs into a bowl and set aside.

Blitz the cooked aubergine and onion in the
food processor until semi-smooth. Add the

breadcrumbs in three stages, blitzing after
each addition, to form a firm mixture. Stir
in the parsley and season well. Allow to cool
for a few minutes.

Heat the remaining 2 tablespoons of oil in
the frying pan over a medium-high heat.
Roll the mixture into walnut-sized balls
and carefully place in the oil. Cook for 3–4
minutes on each side, until golden at the
top and bottom. Remove from the pan,
drain on kitchen paper and keep warm.

To make the marinara sauce, heat the oil
and garlic in a pan over a medium heat for
2 minutes. Pour in the chopped tomatoes
and sugar, then simmer for 8–10 minutes,
stirring often. Remove from the heat, stir
through the parsley, then season to taste.

Serve the no-meat balls alongside the hot
marinara sauce, with spaghetti or loaded
into bread subs.

**GET AHEAD**
The marinara sauce can be made in
advance and frozen. The no-meat
balls are best when cooked fresh,
however the uncooked mix can be
made and chilled one day ahead.

# SICILIAN-STYLE ANTIPASTI PIZZAS

## SERVES 2

Need pizza in a hurry? Look no further than these pizza squares, which are ready from start to finish in under 15 minutes. In true Sicilian style, these pizzas have a thick base and square shape, and are loaded with antipasti tomatoes, olives and (bell) peppers. There's no need for vegan cheese as the preserved toppings will add enough flavour, but if you fancy a sprinkle of vegan cheese, go for it! Serve with a side salad, or with crispy polenta chips (opposite).

4 squares of focaccia bread (ensure
  dairy- and egg-free)
8 tsp tomato purée (paste)
pinch of dried oregano
6 sundried tomatoes in oil, drained
  and sliced
12 pitted green olives, halved
4 jarred (bell) pepper slices in oil, drained
¼ red onion, sliced
generous drizzle of extra virgin olive oil
generous pinch of sea salt and black pepper
few small basil leaves, to garnish

Preheat the oven to 180°C/350°F/gas mark 4.

Arrange the focaccia squares on a baking tray and smooth over 2 teaspoons of tomato purée per square. Scatter with the oregano.

Distribute the sundried tomatos, olives, peppers and red onion over the breads, then drizzle with olive oil.

Bake in the oven for 8–10 minutes until the toppings are hot, then season with sea salt and pepper. Scatter over the basil leaves, then serve hot or cold.

✦ **GET AHEAD**
Ready-made focaccia is available in supermarkets and makes a quick, bready base for homemade pizzas. Do check that they're dairy and egg-free before purchasing.

# ROSEMARY SALT POLENTA CHIPS

## SERVES 2 GENEROUSLY AS A SIDE DISH

Polenta chips are a favourite side dish in many Italian-inspired restaurants, and are super-easy to make at home. Serve with Sicilian-style antipasti pizza (opposite) for an elegant Italian night in.

500g (1lb 2oz) ready-made firm polenta
2 tbsp olive oil
2 sprigs of rosemary, leaves removed and very finely chopped
generous pinch of sea salt

✳

Preheat the oven to 200°C/400°F/gas mark 6.

Slice the firm polenta into thick, even chips about 1.5cm (¾in) thick and arrange evenly on a baking tray.

Drizzle with olive oil and rub the oil over the chips evenly. Scatter with rosemary and sea salt then bake in the oven for 25–30 minutes until the edges are starting to turn golden brown. Serve hot.

### ✦ TAKE-OUT TIP
Ready-made firm polenta is available in large supermarkets, however if you are unable to find firm polenta or would prefer to make your own, simply bring 1.5 litres (6½ cups) of water to the boil in a large saucepan, then add in 400g (2¾ cups) quick-cook fine polenta and a generous pinch of salt. Place over a medium heat and stir constantly for 10 minutes, lowering the heat slightly as it begins to thicken. Line two deep baking trays with baking parchment, then pour the polenta mixture into the trays. Cool for at least 2 hours before slicing.

# FETTUCCINE ALFREDO

## SERVES 2

Creamy and indulgent, fettuccine alfredo is surprisingly simple and quick to make at home. Most dried pasta you find in the supermarket is egg-free, but always check before buying. If you can't source dried fettuccine, tagliatelle is an excellent substitute.

160g (5½oz) dried fettuccine
 (ensure egg-free)
2 tsp sunflower oil
2 garlic cloves, crushed
150ml (generous ½ cup) single soya cream
pinch of freshly grated nutmeg
small handful of flat-leaf parsley,
 finely chopped
generous pinch of sea salt and black pepper

✳

Bring a large a large pan of salted water to the boil and add the fettuccine. Simmer for 8–10 minutes until al dente.

In a separate pan, heat the oil and garlic for 2 minutes until the oil is infused and the garlic has softened.

Pour in the soya cream and simmer for 5 minutes, stirring occasionally. Season to taste with a generous pinch of salt and pepper, then stir through the nutmeg.

Thoroughly drain the fettuccine, then toss the pasta into the creamy sauce. Serve in warm bowls, scatter over the flat-leaf parsley and finish with some more nutmeg and black pepper.

 **GET AHEAD**
The alfredo sauce can be made up to 2 days in advance, when kept refrigerated in a sealed container. The pasta is best cooked fresh just before eating.

# CREAMY LEEK, PEA AND LEMON RISOTTO

## SERVES 2 GENEROUSLY

Are you someone who waits to order risotto at a restaurant, because it seems too tricky to make at home? Let this simple and delicious recipe show you how easy it really is to create an elegant risotto, with just a few ingredients. Don't switch the arborio rice for another type of rice, as this starchy variety is what adds the creaminess.

1 tbsp sunflower oil
1 medium leek, finely chopped
1 garlic clove, crushed
200g (7oz) arborio rice
generous glug of white wine (ensure vegan)
800ml (3½ cups) hot vegetable stock
2 tbsp vegan cream cheese
generous handful of frozen peas
zest and juice of 1 unwaxed lemon
generous pinch of sea salt and black pepper

✳

In a large pan, heat the oil and leek over a medium-high heat for 4–5 minutes until the leek begins to soften. Add the garlic and cook for 1 further minute.

Pour in the rice. Stir for 1–2 minutes until the edges of the rice become transparent. Pour in the white wine and reduce for 2–3 minutes, stirring frequently.

Pour in 200ml (¾ cup) of the vegetable stock and stir constantly for 5–6 minutes until most of the stock has been absorbed.

Reduce to a medium heat then pour in the next 200ml (¾ cup) and cook for a further 5–6 minutes, stirring constantly, then repeat until of all of the stock has been absorbed in 200ml (¾ cup) amounts.

Stir in the vegan cream cheese and frozen peas and cook for a further 5 minutes, continuing to stir to avoid the risotto sticking to the bottom of the pan.

Remove from the heat and stir through the lemon juice. Season to taste with salt and pepper, spoon into warmed bowls and top with some lemon zest.

✦ GET AHEAD

Frozen chopped leeks also work well in this recipe if you are unable to source fresh leeks. You'll find the frozen variety at most supermarkets, alongside the other frozen vegetables.

# CHEAT'S LEMON AND PISTACHIO CANNOLI

## MAKES 8 / SERVES 4

Cannoli are classic Italian sweet snacks, with a sweet case, creamy filling and pistachios. The tubes can be quite tricky to make, so I've created this cheat's version, using baked mini tortilla wraps, flavoured with cinnamon sugar. Choose mild or 'original' flavour vegan cream cheese to make the filling, as this has a similar flavour and texture to mascarpone cheese.

8 mini soft tortilla wraps
2 tsp sunflower oil
1 tsp granulated sugar
½ tsp ground cinnamon
400g (14oz) mild vegan cream cheese
2 tsp good-quality vanilla extract
finely grated zest and juice of 2 unwaxed
    lemons
6 tbsp icing (confectioner's) sugar
4 tbsp shelled pistachios, finely chopped

✳

Preheat the oven to 200°C/400°F/gas mark 6.

Tear off eight 10cm (4in) pieces of foil and roll them into long cylinders. Place one in the centre of each mini tortilla and roll the tortilla around it. The foil cylinders will hold the centres of the tubes open during cooking. Place the tortilla rolls seam side down on a baking tray.

Brush the tortilla rolls all over with sunflower oil. Mix together the sugar and cinnamon and then sprinkle this over the rolls. Bake in the oven for 7–10 minutes,

then carefully remove the tray from the oven and use tongs to turn the rolls over. Return to the oven to bake for a further 3–5 minutes until golden.

Meanwhile, mix together the vegan cream cheese, vanilla extract, lemon zest and juice. Sift in the icing sugar and mix until combined.

Carefully remove the golden cannoli from the oven and allow to cool. Once cool, remove the foil.

Use a teaspoon to fill the cannoli with the lemon cream, or fill a piping bag with the lemon cream and squeeze into the cannoli from each end. Press the chopped pistachios generously onto both ends of each cannoli and serve immediately.

### GET AHEAD
The cannoli shells can be made up to 2 days in advance and kept in an airtight container. Fill the cannoli with the lemon cream just before serving.

# COFFEE AND CREAM PANNA COTTA

## SERVES 2

**Panna cotta is indulgent and creamy, yet light enough to enjoy at the end of any carb-heavy Italian feast. Use good-quality, finely ground instant coffee for the best flavour.**

1 x 400g (14fl oz) can full-fat coconut milk
2 tsp good-quality instant coffee powder
2 tbsp caster (superfine) sugar
2 tsp agar flakes

✳

Pour the coconut milk into a pan and bring to a simmer over a medium heat.

Stir in the coffee and sugar until dissolved, then stir in the agar flakes. Simmer for 4–5 minutes until the agar flakes have dissolved fully.

Pour the mixture into small panna cotta moulds, then refrigerate for at least 6 hours until set.

Remove the panna cotta from the fridge and place the containers in a bowl of hot water for up to a minute, to make them easier to unmould. Place the panna cotta moulds upside down on serving plates and gently shake to allow the panna cotta to slide onto the plates. Serve immediately.

✦ **TAKE-OUT TIP**

Agar is a vegan alternative to gelatine, made from seaweed. It will set the panna cotta and give it that all-important wobble! You'll find agar flakes in large supermarkets, in the baking section or world food aisle.

# MENU FOR 4

You can never go wrong with an Indian-style feast. Creamy curries, spices as hot as you can handle, and those decadent desserts – these delicacies are as simple to make at home as they are to eat, but with the reassurance that everything you've cooked is 100 per cent vegan!

# EASIEST-EVER PESHWARI NAANS

## MAKES 4

Nothing beats a warm naan bread to mop up curry sauce, only perfected with the addition of coconut and sultanas (golden raisins) in these easiest-ever Peshwari naans. They contain no yeast, have no proving time, and can be ready in moments. You'll wonder how you ever enjoyed an Indian-style feast without this recipe! I love to serve these alongside some extra coconut yogurt for dipping.

**Suitable for freezing**

200g (generous 1½ cups) self-raising flour,
   plus extra for dusting
½ tsp baking powder
½ tsp granulated sugar
4 tbsp coconut yogurt
2 tbsp sunflower oil
2 tbsp desiccated coconut
1 tbsp sultanas (golden raisins)
2 tsp vegan butter, for brushing

✳

In a large bowl, stir together the flour, baking powder and sugar. Spoon in the yogurt, oil, desiccated coconut and sultanas, and bring together to form a dough.

Lightly dust a clean surface with flour, then knead the dough for 2 minutes. Cut the dough into 4 even balls, then use the palm of your hand to flatten them into circles, making them slightly thicker at the edges than at the centre.

Heat a dry frying pan (skillet) over a high heat, then carefully place in the flattened dough circles, two at a time. Cook for 4–5 minutes on each side, turning with tongs, until brown patches appear on the bread.

Remove the naans from the pan and use a pastry brush to liberally spread the butter over each side. Serve warm.

**TAKE-OUT TIP**

Use coconut yogurt with no added sugar in these naans for an extra tangy flavour. You'll find this in most large supermarkets. You can freeze these before brushing with butter; once defrosted, reheat thoroughly in a dry pan and brush with butter as above.

# CANDY-STRIPE ONION BHAJIS

## SERVES 4 AS A SIDE DISH OR STARTER

Who knew that homemade bhajis were so easy? Just when you thought this Indian classic couldn't get any better, the combination of both red and standard white onions creates a striped effect beneath the golden outer. Swirling a spoonful of coconut yogurt through some mango chutney makes the perfect dip for these delicious bhajis.

500ml (generous 2 cups) sunflower oil, for frying
5 tbsp plain (all-purpose) flour
1 tsp ground cumin
1 tsp garam masala
½ tsp chilli powder
1 tsp sea salt, crushed
1 red onion, thinly sliced
1 onion, thinly sliced
small handful of coriander (cilantro), finely chopped

✳

Begin to heat the oil in a large, heavy-based pan over a medium-high heat.

In a large bowl, mix together the flour, cumin, garam masala, chilli powder and salt. Throw in all of the onion slices, then stir to coat the slices in the dry mixture. Stir through 3 tablespoons of cold water to form a thick, even mixture.

Test if the oil is hot enough by dripping a small amount of batter into the pan; it should sizzle, rise and become golden. Working in batches, carefully spoon tablespoon-sized amounts of the mixture into the hot oil and cook for 4–5 minutes until golden. Use a slotted spoon to remove the bhajis and drain on kitchen paper before scattering with the coriander and serving.

**TAKE-OUT TIP**
Cook 3–4 bhajis at a time to ensure they don't stick to each other in the pan.

# SAAG ALOO

**This popular side dish of potatoes and spinach is a staple on Indian restaurant menus, and is so simple to make at home. New potatoes are perfectly waxy, easy to prepare and become beautifully infused with spices.**

10 new potatoes, rinsed clean
1 tbsp sunflower oil
1 onion, finely diced
1 garlic clove, crushed
1cm (½in) piece of fresh ginger, peeled and grated
1 tsp garam masala
1 tsp cumin seeds
1 tsp mustard seeds
½ tsp ground turmeric
½ tsp mild chilli powder
4 generous handfuls of spinach leaves
generous pinch of sea salt

Bring a large pan of water to the boil over a medium-high heat, then carefully add the new potatoes. Boil for 20–25 minutes until softened, then drain. Slice each potato in half and set aside.

Add the oil to the pan, along with the onion, garlic and ginger. Soften over a medium heat for 3–4 minutes.

Add the garam masala, cumin and mustard seeds, turmeric and chilli powder, then cook for a further 3–4 minutes, stirring frequently to avoid the spices burning.

Stir in the cooked potatoes, along with 150ml (generous ½ cup) hot water and the spinach leaves. Cook down for 5 minutes, stirring often until the potatoes are coated and the spinach has wilted.

Remove from the heat and season to taste with a generous pinch of sea salt.

### ✦ GET AHEAD
Cook the new potatoes up to 2 days in advance, allow to cool, then refrigerate until required. Canned new potatoes also make an excellent alternative – no need to pre-cook!

# PERFECT PILAU RICE

## SERVES 4 AS A SIDE DISH

**Every Indian-style spread needs a side of fluffy, fragrant pilau rice.
And it's easier to cook at home than you think!**

300g (10oz) basmati rice
500ml (generous 2 cups) hot
  vegetable stock
½ tsp ground turmeric
1 cinnamon stick
2 bay leaves

*

Add all of the ingredients to a large pan
and bring to a simmer over a medium heat.
Cook for 15 minutes, stirring occasionally
to avoid sticking.

When all of the stock has been absorbed,
remove the pan from the heat, then cover
with a lid. Leave to stand for 5 minutes.

Remove the cinnamon stick and bay
leaves, and discard. Fork through the rice
to separate the strands. Serve hot.

**✦ TAKE-OUT TIP**
To make the rice go a little further,
and for a fruity flavour twist, stir
through some desiccated coconut
and plump sultanas (golden raisins)
before serving.

# SAMOSADILLA

### SERVES 2 AS A SIDE DISH OR STARTER

**Welcome the king of fusion – the samosa quesadilla. Sandwich Indian-spiced vegetables between soft tortillas and cook on a griddle pan, Mexican-style. Serve hot with mango chutney, for dipping.**

1 tbsp sunflower oil, plus 1 tsp for drizzling
1 carrot, peeled and grated
6 green beans, roughly chopped
2 spring onions (scallions), finely chopped
handful of frozen peas
handful of frozen or canned sweetcorn
1 tsp garam masala
juice of ½ unwaxed lime
generous pinch of sea salt
2 large soft tortilla wraps

✳

Heat the oil in a large frying pan (skillet) over a high heat, add the carrot, green beans and spring onions and cook for 3–4 minutes, stirring frequently. Add the peas, sweetcorn and garam masala and cook for a further minute.

Stir through the lime juice and salt and cook for 1–2 minutes.

Meanwhile, rub the remaining teaspoon of oil over the surface of a griddle (grill) pan, then place over a high heat.

Spread the spiced filling over one half of each tortilla, fold in half tightly, then carefully place on the hot griddle pan for 3–4 minutes until griddle lines appear, then flip to cook the other side for 2–3 minutes.

Carefully remove from the pan and cut each folded tortilla in half before serving.

 **TAKE-OUT TIP**
Samosadilla tastes great hot, but makes an equally great cold lunch, if you have any leftovers.

# CARAMELIZED ONION DHAL

## SERVES 4

**No Indian spread is complete without a comforting lentil dhal. This version includes caramelized onions, for subtle sweetness with minimal effort, all in one pan! Serve as a simple side dish, or as a satisfying main dish with basmati rice.**

2 tbsp sunflower oil
2 onions, thinly sliced
2 garlic cloves, crushed
1 tsp ground turmeric
1 tsp ground cumin
½ tsp dried chilli flakes
1 tbsp medium curry paste (ensure dairy-free)
300g (10oz) dried red lentils
1 litre (4 cups) hot vegetable stock
handful of flat-leaf parsley, finely chopped
generous pinch of sea salt

✳

Heat the oil in a large pan over a medium-high heat, add the sliced onions and cook for 8–10 minutes, stirring occasionally to prevent sticking, until the onions are golden brown. Remove half of the cooked onions from the pan, and set them aside.

Add the garlic, turmeric, cumin and chilli flakes to the remaining onions in the pan and cook for 1 minute. Then stir in the curry paste until combined.

Pour in the red lentils and half of the stock, then simmer over a medium heat for 10 minutes. After 10 minutes, add the remaining stock and simmer until the liquid has been absorbed, stirring frequently to avoid sticking.

Remove from the heat and stir through the reserved caramelized onions and the parsley. Season to taste with sea salt. Serve hot.

✦ **TAKE-OUT TIP**

Any remaining dhal can be turned into soup the following day! Simply add some extra stock and blitz until smooth. The dhal is also great if made a day in advance.

# ALL-IN-ONE BIRYANI

## SERVES 4

This family favourite combines gentle spices, cashews, coconut milk and fluffy rice for an all-in-one dish that is ready in under an hour. I love the mix of vegetables used here, but feel free to use any vegetables that you have available at home.

400g (14oz) basmati rice
2 carrots, peeled and sliced into rounds
½ head of cauliflower, broken into florets
10 green beans, trimmed and halved
2 tbsp frozen or canned sweetcorn
generous handful of cashew nuts
1 x 400ml (14fl oz) can coconut milk
1 tbsp medium curry paste (ensure
  dairy-free)
1 tsp ground turmeric
½ tsp ground cumin
½ tsp dried chilli flakes
2 spring onions (scallions), finely sliced
generous handful of coriander (cilantro),
  roughly torn
generous pinch of sea salt
juice of ½ unwaxed lemon, plus lemon
  wedges to serve

✳

Preheat the oven to 200°C/400°F/
gas mark 6.

Scatter the rice into a deep baking tray, along with the carrots, cauliflower florets, green beans, sweetcorn and cashews.

Pour the coconut milk into a jug, along with 200ml (generous ¾ cup) cold water. Whisk in the curry paste, turmeric, cumin and chilli flakes until combined.

Pour the spiced coconut milk mix over the rice and gently stir through to ensure all of the rice is coated.

Loosely cover the baking tray with foil, then bake in the oven for 45–50 minutes until the coconut milk has been absorbed by the rice and the vegetables have softened.

Carefully remove the tray from the oven and remove the foil. Scatter over the spring onions and coriander, then season with sea salt and lemon juice. Serve hot with wedges of lemon.

**GET AHEAD**
You can prepare the carrots, cauliflower and green beans up to a day ahead, then refrigerate for freshness.

# BUTTER CHICKPEAS

## SERVES 2 GENEROUSLY

This mild and saucy chickpea curry is creamy and addictive, and just made for dipping. The sauce quantity is large, which is perfect for mopping up with homemade naan breads (page 74). Friday night doesn't get much more comforting than this.

**Suitable for freezing**

1 tbsp sunflower oil
1 onion, finely diced
1 garlic clove, crushed
1 tsp ginger purée
1 tsp ground cumin
½ tsp dried chilli flakes
1 tbsp mild curry paste (ensure dairy-free)
2 heaped tbsp tomato purée (paste)
1 x 400ml (14fl oz) can full-fat coconut milk
2 x 400g (14oz) cans chickpeas, thoroughly drained and rinsed
3 tbsp coconut yogurt
generous pinch of sea salt and black pepper

Heat the sunflower oil in a large pan, add the onion and cook over a high heat for 2 minutes until the onion begins to soften.

Add the garlic, ginger purée, cumin, chilli flakes, curry paste and tomato purée and stir through for 1 minute.

Pour in the coconut milk and chickpeas, then cook for 10–12 minutes, stirring occasionally, until the sauce is creamy.

Remove from the heat and lightly stir in the coconut yogurt. Season to taste with sea salt and black pepper and serve immediately.

### GET AHEAD
This curry freezes well so is a good one for batch cooking, although it's best to reserve the cooling coconut yogurt until just before serving as it can separate a little during the freezing process.

# ROASTED AUBERGINE JALFREZI

## SERVES 2

Create this Indian classic in 30 minutes, with minimal fuss and using basic store cupboard ingredients. The aubergine (eggplant) and cherry tomatoes become addictively sweet and sticky when roasted, offering a delicious contrast to the spicy curry sauce. Add more or less green chilli depending on how hot you like it!

**Suitable for freezing**

1 large aubergine (eggplant), sliced into long quarters, then each quarter sliced lengthways again
10 cherry tomatoes
2 tbsp sunflower oil
1 onion, finely diced
2 garlic cloves, crushed
1 tsp ginger purée
2 green chillies, thinly sliced into rings
1 tbsp garam masala
1 tsp ground turmeric
1 tsp ground cumin
1 x 400g (14oz) can chopped tomatoes
1 tsp sugar
generous pinch of sea salt
small handful of coriander (cilantro) leaves, roughly torn

✳

Preheat the oven to 200°C/400°F/ gas mark 6.

Arrange the sliced aubergines and cherry tomatoes on a baking tray and drizzle with 1 tablespoon of the sunflower oil. Roast in the oven for 30 minutes until the aubergine is tender and the tomatoes are slightly browned.

In the meantime, make the jalfrezi base. In a large pan, heat the remaining tablespoon of oil and the onion over a medium heat for 2–3 minutes until the onion has begun to soften, then add the garlic, ginger purée and half the sliced chillies, cooking for a further 1–2 minutes.

Add the garam masala, turmeric and cumin and stir through for 1 minute. Pour in the chopped tomatoes and sugar, then simmer for 20 minutes, stirring occasionally.

Carefully remove the roasted aubergines and cherry tomatoes from the oven, and use tongs to place them over the jalfrezi sauce. Season with sea salt, then scatter over remaining green chilli and the coriander leaves just before serving.

✦ **GET AHEAD**

This curry freezes well, so you can simply defrost and thoroughly reheat before enjoying.

# CREAMY BUTTERBEAN KORMA

## SERVES 4

Korma is one of the UK's most popular curries, with a delicately spiced, creamy base that doesn't leave you reaching for that glass of water. This recipe proves that korma doesn't have to be a bland dish, with toasted almonds, creamy coconut milk, plump sultanas (golden raisins) and a swirl of cooling yogurt. Serve with fluffy basmati rice (page 80) or homemade naan breads (page 74).

**Suitable for freezing**

2 tbsp flaked (slivered) almonds
1 tbsp sunflower oil
1 onion, diced
1 garlic clove, crushed
1 tsp ginger purée
1 tsp ground turmeric
1 tbsp mild curry paste (ensure dairy-free)
1 x 400ml (14fl oz) can coconut milk
1 x 400g (14oz) can butterbeans, drained and thoroughly rinsed
1 tbsp mango chutney
1 tbsp sultanas (golden raisins)
generous handful of spinach leaves
1 tbsp unsweetened coconut yogurt
small handful of coriander (cilantro) leaves, roughly chopped
generous pinch of sea salt

✳

In a dry pan, toast the flaked almonds over a high heat for 2–3 minutes until golden, shaking the pan frequently to prevent them burning. Tip the toasted almonds into a bowl and set aside.

Add the oil and onion to a large pan and cook over a medium-high heat for 2–3 minutes until the onion has begun to soften. Add the garlic, ginger purée, turmeric and curry paste and stir through for a minute.

Pour in the coconut milk and butterbeans, then simmer for 10 minutes, stirring occasionally. Spoon in the mango chutney, sultanas and spinach, then cook for a further 5 minutes.

Remove the pan from the heat and lightly swirl through the coconut yogurt. Scatter over the coriander leaves with the reserved toasted almonds. Season to taste with sea salt. Serve hot.

✦ **GET AHEAD**

This curry is perfect for freezing in individual portions, for when you need fast food with no effort. Add the coriander (cilantro) leaves and coconut yogurt when the portions have been thoroughly reheated.

# TIKKA CAULIFLOWER SKEWERS

## SERVES 4

**Oven-baked, spiced, and easy to make – could an Indian-style classic be any more tempting? Top with coriander (cilantro), red chilli and a squeeze of lemon juice to take it to the next level. Serve on a bed of fluffy basmati rice.**

250g (9oz) unsweetened soya yogurt
1 tbsp medium curry paste (ensure
  dairy-free)
½ tsp ground turmeric
½ tsp chilli powder
1 head of cauliflower, broken into about
  32 bite-sized florets
juice of ¼ unwaxed lemon
1 red chilli, deseeded and thinly sliced
small handful of coriander (cilantro)
  leaves, torn
pinch of sea salt

✳

Preheat the oven to 200°C/400°F/gas mark 6 and soak 8 wooden kebab skewers in cold water.

In a large bowl, whisk together the soya yogurt, curry paste, turmeric and chilli powder until combined. Dip the cauliflower

florets into the yogurt mix, coating them completely. Do this in batches to ensure an even coverage.

Thread the cauliflower florets onto the soaked kebab skewers, about 4 on each skewer, and place on a couple of baking trays. Bake in the oven for 25–30 minutes until the florets have softened and are starting to char.

Carefully remove from the oven and squeeze over the lemon juice. Scatter with chilli and coriander leaves, then season with a pinch of salt.

 **GET AHEAD**
The cauliflower florets can be coated in tikka yogurt a day before baking; simply keep refrigerated in an airtight container.

# VINDALOO

## SERVES 4

This one is for the heat lovers among you. Pop the ingredients for this fiery vindaloo in your slow cooker and let it cook itself while you get on with your day. Then return to a hot, zippy curry, for maximum enjoyment with minimal effort. Serve with a Mango and lime lassi (page 96).

1 tbsp sunflower oil
2 tsp hot curry powder
1 tsp ground cumin
1 tsp ground turmeric
½ tsp dried chilli flakes
2 garlic cloves, crushed
1 onion, diced
1 courgette (zucchini), evenly diced
generous handful of green beans, trimmed
1 green (bell) pepper, deseeded and
    thinly sliced
8 small florets of broccoli
handful of frozen peas
1–2 green chillies, seeds left in,
    thinly sliced
500g (1lb 2oz) passata
1 heaped tbsp tomato purée (paste)
1 tbsp malt vinegar
handful of coriander (cilantro) leaves,
    roughly torn
generous pinch of sea salt

✳

Preheat the slow cooker by setting it to low.

In a bowl, mix together the oil, curry powder, cumin, turmeric, chilli flakes and garlic to form a spice paste.

Add the onion, courgette, green beans, green pepper, broccoli and peas to the slow cooker, then stir in the chillies, reserving a few slices to garnish before serving.

Pour in the passata, tomato purée and vinegar, then stir through the spice paste.

Place the lid on the slow cooker, then cook on low for 6 hours until the vegetables are tender.

Scatter over the reserved chilli slices, then stir through the coriander and season to taste with sea salt.

 **TAKE-OUT TIP**
The intensity of heat from the chillies increases with each mouthful, which is worth bearing in mind when deciding to add more chilli (note that the seeds are left in). Have a tub of chilled coconut yogurt at the ready for serving!

# MANGO AND LIME LASSI

## SERVES 4

**No Indian-style feast is complete without a drink of creamy lassi to cool and comfort. Serve with Vindaloo (page 95), or as a sweet end to any spicy meal.**

500g (1lb 2oz) coconut yogurt, chilled
1 ripe mango, peeled, stoned and diced into
 rough chunks
1 tbsp maple syrup
juice of 1 unwaxed lime
ice cubes, to fill 4 tall glasses

✳

Add the coconut yogurt, mango, maple syrup and lime juice to a high-powered jug blender, then blitz on high until completely smooth.

Fill four tall glasses with ice, then pour the smooth lassi over. Serve immediately.

### GET AHEAD

A high-powered jug blender will blitz the mango in no time, but if you only have a hand-held stick blender, simply add the ingredients to a jug and spend a little longer blending until smooth.

# COCONUT KHEER PUDDING

## SERVES 4

Creamy kheer is the perfect end to your Indian-inspired meal.
Imagine the creamiest rice pudding, with gentle spices and nuts –
hot, comforting and ready in 30 minutes.

1 x 400ml (14fl oz) can full-fat
  coconut milk
2 tbsp granulated sugar
2 tbsp desiccated coconut
¼ tsp grated nutmeg
¼ tsp ground cinnamon
pinch of ground cardamom
100g (3½oz) basmati rice
1 tbsp flaked (slivered) almonds
1 tbsp shelled pistachios, roughly chopped

✳

Add the coconut milk to a large pan then
fill the empty can up with hot water and
pour this into the pan too. Bring to a
simmer over a medium heat, then add
the sugar, desiccated coconut, nutmeg,
cinnamon and cardamom.

Stir in the basmati rice and cook for
20–25 minutes, stirring frequently to
avoid sticking.

Remove the pan from the heat and stir
through the flaked almonds. Spoon into
warmed bowls and scatter with chopped
pistachios.

**✦ TAKE-OUT TIP**
Full-fat coconut milk will give the
creamiest texture, so save any
reduced-fat versions for another
recipe.

# CHIN

## MENU FOR 2

Demystify what appears like complicated cuisine, and cook up a Chinese feast in the comfort of your own kitchen. Chinese food is the most common food to get delivered: with addictively slippery noodles, tastes of sweet, hot and sour sauce, and those all-important sides, who can blame us?

IESE

# HOT AND SOUR SOUP

## SERVES 4 GENEROUSLY

**The perfect start to any Chinese feast, this soup will stimulate your taste buds and awaken your senses with a hit of fresh chilli, savoury soy sauce and sour vinegar, which for me must always be malt. Serve with chopsticks for the vegetables and tofu, and a spoon for the broth.**

**Suitable for freezing**

1 tbsp sunflower oil
1 carrot, peeled and cut into matchsticks
2 spring onions (scallions), thinly sliced
1 red chilli, deseeded and thinly sliced
2 garlic cloves, crushed
1 tbsp ginger purée
4 leaves of savoy cabbage, thinly sliced
150g (5oz) beansprouts
1 x 225g (8oz) can water chestnuts, thoroughly drained and rinsed
1 litre (4 cups) hot vegetable stock
1 tbsp tomato purée (paste)
100g (3½oz) firm tofu, drained and diced into small chunks
1 tbsp malt vinegar
1 tbsp dark soy sauce
handful of chives, finely chopped, plus extra to garnish
handful of coriander (cilantro), roughly chopped

✳

Heat the oil in a large pan over a high heat, then throw in the carrot, spring onions and chilli. Stir-fry for 2–3 minutes, then add the garlic, ginger and cabbage and cook for a further minute.

Add the contents of the pan to a slow cooker, along with the beansprouts, water chestnuts and stock. Spoon in the tomato purée and stir. Simmer for 3–4 hours until the vegetables become tender.

Add the tofu and cook for a further 30 minutes.

Turn off the slow cooker and stir through the vinegar, soy sauce, chives and coriander. Ladle into warmed bowls and scatter with some more chives to serve.

 **GET AHEAD**
There's no need to press the tofu for this recipe; simply chop into small chunks for soft bites with every mouthful of soup. This soup freezes well – transfer to a freezer-proof container before adding the fresh herbs. Once defrosted thoroughly, reheat and then stir in the chopped chives and coriander.

# CRISPY KALE
# SEAWEED

### SERVES 2 AS A SIDE DISH

**Did you know that the crispy seaweed in your usual Chinese order is actually fried kale or spring greens? It's called seaweed because the finished dish really does look like seaweed! This version is baked, for all the crisp texture without the extra fat.**

180g (6oz) shredded kale, tough stems discarded
2 tbsp sunflower oil
1 tsp granulated sugar
½ tsp sea salt
generous pinch of Chinese five-spice
2 tsp sesame seeds

✳

Preheat the oven to 180°C/350°F/gas mark 4.

In a large bowl, mix together the kale and oil, then scatter through the sugar, sea salt, Chinese five-spice and sesame seeds. Stir through to evenly distribute.

Lay the kale out evenly across two baking trays. Bake in the oven for 9–10 minutes until crisp. Serve hot.

### ✦ GET AHEAD

Use a bag of pre-chopped kale for this recipe to save you time chopping large leaves, meaning this side dish can be ready from start to finish in under 15 minutes!

# HONG KONG-STYLE SWEET AND SOUR CAULIFLOWER

### SERVES 2

Just when you think the classic *sweet and sour* can't get any better
– top with deep-fried, battered cauliflower for a version that is
popular in Hong Kong. Serve with Extra fried rice (page 110).

**For the cauliflower**
100g (scant 1 cup) self-raising flour
100g (¾ cup) cornflour (cornstarch)
500ml (generous 2 cups) sunflower oil,
　for frying
1 small cauliflower, broken into bite-sized
　florets, stems trimmed

**For the sweet and sour sauce**
1 tbsp sunflower oil
1 green (bell) pepper, roughly sliced
5 baby corns, roughly sliced in half
1 x 400g (14oz) can pineapple chunks,
　drained
150g (5oz) tomato ketchup
50g (2oz) soft light brown sugar
5 tbsp malt vinegar
1 tbsp light soy sauce
small handful of coriander (cilantro),
　roughly torn

✴

In a large bowl, mix together the flour and
cornflour, then whisk in 150ml (generous
½ cup) cold water until a smooth batter is
formed. Allow to stand for a few minutes,
while you heat the oil in a large heavy-
based pan or a deep fryer.

Check if the oil is hot enough by dropping
in a blob of the batter – if it sizzles
immediately, the oil is ready. Dip the
cauliflower florets into the batter, then use
a slotted spoon to lower a few florets into
the hot oil. Fry for 3–4 minutes until light
golden. Don't overload the pan, it's better
to fry the cauliflower in batches. Drain on
kitchen paper, then keep warm.

To make the sweet and sour sauce, heat the
oil in a wok over a high heat, then throw
in the pepper, baby corns and pineapple
chunks; stir-fry for 2 minutes. Add the
tomato ketchup, brown sugar, vinegar and
soy sauce, then stir-fry for 8–10 minutes
until the sauce has thickened and the
vegetables have softened.

Spoon the sauce and vegetables onto
plates, then top with the battered
cauliflower. Sprinkle with coriander and
serve immediately.

✦　**GET AHEAD**
　Make the sweet and sour sauce up to
　2 days in advance. Keep refrigerated
　in an airtight container, then reheat
　thoroughly before serving with the
　freshly battered and fried cauliflower.

# CRISPY VEGETABLE SPRING ROLLS

**SERVES 4**

Get all the flavour and crunch of spring rolls, without having to fry them!
Use just one sheet of filo pastry for each spring roll for optimum crunch,
then oven bake to create your favourite Chinese side dish. Serve with a
small bowl of soy sauce or sweet chilli, for seriously addictive dipping.

1 tbsp sunflower oil
2 carrots, peeled and sliced into ribbons
  using a vegetable peeler
2 spring onions (scallions), finely chopped
2 radishes, diced
small handful of kale
½ tsp Chinese five-spice
8 sheets of filo pastry (ensure dairy-free)
2 tsp sesame seeds

✳

Preheat the oven to 200°C/400°F/gas
mark 6 and line a baking sheet with baking
parchment.

In a wok, heat the oil over a high heat.
Throw in the carrot ribbons, spring onions,
radishes and kale, then stir-fry for 3–4
minutes until the vegetables start to
soften. Scatter in the Chinese five-spice
and stir-fry for a further minute. Leave to
cool slightly.

Carefully unroll the pastry sheets on a flat
surface. With the short side of a pastry
sheet in front of you, spoon a tablespoon-
sized amount of the vegetable filling into
a line about 10cm (4in) long, along the
centre of the bottom edge. Fold both sides
in to cover the filling, then start rolling
from the bottom all the way to the end of
the pastry sheet to encase the vegetables
in the pastry. Place the spring roll on the
baking sheet and repeat with the remaining
pastry sheets and filling.

Press the sesame seeds onto the tops of
the spring rolls, then bake in the oven for
20–25 minutes until golden and crisp.

 **TAKE-OUT TIP**
Many brands of shop-bought filo
pastry are accidentally vegan, as they
use vegetable oil instead of butter,
but always read the label before
purchasing.

# EXTRA FRIED RICE

## SERVES 2

A Chinese feast is never complete without a generous side of extra fried rice. This version is loaded with vegetables, edamame beans and a hint of spice, along with the classic flavours of sesame oil and soy sauce.

1 tbsp sunflower oil
handful of frozen or fresh podded
   edamame beans
small handful of frozen peas
2 spring onions (scallions), finely chopped
1 carrot, peeled and finely diced
10 sugarsnap peas, halved diagonally
2 tbsp cashew nuts
¼ tsp Chinese five-spice
250g (9oz) cooked long grain rice
2 tbsp dark soy sauce
1 tbsp sesame oil
juice of ½ unwaxed lime

✳

Heat the oil over a high heat in a wok, then throw in the edamame beans, peas, spring onions, carrot and sugarsnap peas. Stir-fry for 3–4 minutes until the vegetables begin to soften.

Stir in the cashews and Chinese five-spice and cook for a further minute.

Add the cooked rice, soy sauce and sesame oil, then stir-fry for a further 2 minutes, to distribute the sauce evenly through the rice and vegetables.

Remove from the heat and stir in the lime juice. Serve hot.

 **GET AHEAD**
Pre-cook the rice up to a day in advance, allow to cool completely, then keep in the fridge until ready to use. Alternatively, use a packet of cooked long grain rice available from supermarkets.

# BLACK BEAN TOFU

## SERVES 4

Black bean sauce feels like a delicious secret, with the recipe mysteriously held by Chinese restaurants – but it is actually so simple to make at home! The secret to success is sourcing the correct beans; you'll need fermented black soy beans, rather than the black beans that you'd use in Mexican-style dishes. Look for them in Chinese supermarkets, online, or in the world food aisle of large supermarkets. Serve over crisp tofu, green (bell) peppers and shredded cabbage, for an authentic Eastern taste.

**Black bean sauce suitable for freezing**

**For the black bean sauce**
1 tbsp sunflower oil
3 garlic cloves, crushed
1 tbsp ginger purée
3 spring onions (scallions), finely chopped
3 tbsp fermented black soy beans, rinsed and roughly chopped
1 heaped tbsp cornflour (cornstarch)

**For the tofu**
1 tbsp cornflour (cornstarch)
280g (9½oz) block of extra-firm tofu, drained and pressed (see page 14), cut into 5cm (2in) slices
1 tbsp sunflower oil
1 green (bell) pepper, thinly sliced
¼ savoy cabbage, roughly sliced

✳

To make the black bean sauce, add the oil, garlic, ginger and 2 of the chopped spring onions to a pan and cook over a medium heat for 2–3 minutes, stirring frequently.

Add the black beans and cook for another minute. Pour in 300ml (1¼ cups) boiling water and the cornflour. Simmer for 15–20 minutes, whisking frequently to form a thick, aromatic sauce.

In the meantime, prepare the tofu. Scatter the cornflour on a plate and dip the tofu slices in to coat them. Heat the oil in a large wok, then carefully add the tofu, cooking for 5–6 minutes on each side until golden. Add the pepper and cabbage and stir-fry for 3–4 minutes until softened. Pour the black bean sauce into the wok and stir to coat everything, cooking for a minute. Scatter over the remaining spring onion and serve.

**GET AHEAD**
Tofu requires draining and pressing to give it a firmer texture. See page 14 for detailed instructions on how to do this. Make extra black bean sauce, place in a freezer-proof container and keep in the freezer for whenever you fancy a Chinese.

# STICKY ORANGE AND SESAME TOFU STUFFED PANCAKES

**SERVES 4**

This sticky orange tofu dish has a hint of chilli, crisp sesame seeds and a topping of crunchy, vibrant spring onions (scallions). Load into pancakes for a tasty version of this restaurant classic that all of the family will love. Have fun experimenting with extra toppings; bean sprouts add a lovely crunch and chives or mint enhance freshness.

**For the pancakes**
150g (1¼ cups) plain (all-purpose) flour,
    plus extra for dusting
1 tsp sunflower oil

**For the tofu**
1 tbsp cornflour (cornstarch)
280g (9½oz) block of extra-firm tofu,
    drained and pressed (see page 14),
    cut into bite-sized chunks
1 tbsp sunflower oil
½ tsp dried chilli flakes
3 tbsp orange marmalade
2 tbsp sesame seeds
2 spring onions (scallions), finely sliced
generous pinch of sea salt

✳

To make the pancakes, add the flour to a bowl, then pour in 120ml (½ cup) boiling water. Stir together to form a thick dough, then allow the dough to rest for 10 minutes until it is cool enough for you to comfortably handle.

Lightly dust a clean work surface with flour, then knead the dough for 5 minutes. Cut the dough into 8 even pieces. Lightly dust a rolling pin with flour, then roll each piece into a circle as thin as possible.

Use a pastry brush to grease a frying pan (skillet) lightly with oil, then place over a medium-high heat. Carefully add each pancake to the pan, cooking for 30 seconds before flipping and cooking for another 30 seconds, ensuring each pancake doesn't brown. Keep warmed.

Dust the cornflour evenly on a plate. Roll the tofu pieces in the cornflour, coating evenly.

Add the oil to a separate frying pan and throw in the tofu. Cook over a high heat for 10–12 minutes, turning the tofu frequently to ensure even cooking. Sprinkle in the chilli flakes and cook for a further minute. Spoon in the marmalade and cook for 2 minutes, stirring continuously. Remove from the heat and scatter with the sesame seeds and spring onions. Season to taste with sea salt. Spoon the tofu into the pancakes just before serving.

**✦ GET AHEAD**

Make these homemade pancakes a few hours in advance and reheat before enjoying, or reduce the overall time of this dish by using shop-bought Chinese-style pancakes, which can be found in large supermarkets.

# SINGAPORE NOODLES

## SERVES 2

Unlike other many other noodle dishes, Singapore noodles are less greasy to eat and have a hint of spice. This dish is ready in under 15 minutes, for when you just fancy some spicy, veg-packed noodles. Ready-to-wok, egg-free noodles can be found in most supermarkets, usually in the Chinese food section (noodles kept in the chilled section are more likely to contain egg), but always check the ingredients before purchasing.

300g (10oz) ready-to-wok soft noodles (ensure egg-free)
1 tbsp sunflower oil
2 tbsp cashew nuts
6 florets of Tenderstem broccoli
handful of mushrooms, brushed clean and halved
8 sugarsnap peas, halved diagonally
2 tsp mild curry powder
¼ tsp ground turmeric
2 tsp light soy sauce
1 spring onion (scallion), thinly sliced
1 small green chilli, deseeded and thinly sliced
small handful of coriander (cilantro) leaves, roughly torn
juice of ¼ unwaxed lemon

✳

Place the noodles in a heatproof bowl, then pour over enough hot water to cover them. Allow them to stand for 4–5 minutes until they are easy to separate, then carefully drain away the hot water.

Heat the oil in a large wok over a high heat. Throw in the cashews, broccoli, mushrooms and sugarsnap peas, then stir-fry for 3–4 minutes until the vegetables appear vibrant in colour. Stir in the curry powder and turmeric.

Add the drained noodles and stir-fry for another 2–3 minutes until the noodles are coated in the spices. Spoon in the soy sauce and cook for 1 further minute.

Remove from the heat and scatter through the spring onion, chilli and coriander. Squeeze over the lemon juice, then serve hot.

 **GET AHEAD**
The vegetables can be chopped and kept up to a day ahead when stored in an airtight container in the fridge.

# SPEEDY SATAY
# STIR-FRY

## SERVES 2

Quicker than a delivery, and a lot cheaper too, this satay stir-fry will hit the spot with a smooth peanut sauce, red chilli and crisp vegetables. Serve over simple steamed rice, or throw in some egg-free noodles while cooking the vegetables in a wok.

**For the stir-fry**
1 tbsp sunflower oil
1 carrot, peeled and thinly sliced
1 medium courgette (zucchini), sliced into
   fine matchsticks
6 sugarsnap peas, sliced diagonally
6 baby corns, sliced diagonally
4 leaves of cavolo nero, roughly chopped
1 red chilli, deseeded and thinly sliced
1 tbsp salted peanuts, roughly chopped
juice of ½ unwaxed lime
2 spring onions (scallions), finely chopped
small handful of coriander (cilantro),
   roughly torn

**For the satay sauce**
2 heaped tbsp smooth peanut butter
1 tbsp dark soy sauce

＊

Heat the oil in a wok over a high heat.
Throw in the carrot, courgette, sugarsnap

peas, baby corns and cavolo nero, then stir-fry for 3–4 minutes. Stir in the chilli and peanuts and cook for 1 further minute.

Meanwhile, put the peanut butter and soy sauce into a jug, then pour in 200ml (generous ¾ cup) hot water. Use a balloon whisk to mix until combined.

Pour the peanut sauce into the wok and stir through for 1–2 minutes, making sure all of the vegetables are coated.

Remove the wok from the heat and squeeze over the lime juice. Scatter over the spring onions and coriander. Serve hot.

**TAKE-OUT TIP**
No cavolo nero available? Savoy cabbage or kale make excellent substitutes.

# CARROT AND CASHEW CHINESE CURRY

## SERVES 4

Tender carrots, crunchy water chestnuts, creamy cashews and that silky sauce. When you fancy a Chinese-style curry, let this one-pot recipe make dinner easy! If you have any leftovers, add some extra vegetable stock and blitz in a blender until smooth, for a delicious soup for the following day.

1 tbsp sunflower oil
3 carrots, peeled and sliced on the diagonal
10 sugarsnap peas
2 spring onions (scallions), roughly chopped
2 tbsp cashew nuts
2 garlic cloves, crushed
1 tsp ginger purée
2 tbsp mild curry powder
1 tsp Chinese five-spice
½ tsp dried chilli flakes
1 tbsp light soy sauce
800ml (3½ cups) hot vegetable stock
2 tbsp cornflour (cornstarch)
1 x 225g (8oz) can water chestnuts, thoroughly drained and rinsed
handful of frozen peas
small handful of coriander (cilantro) leaves

✳

Heat the oil in a large pan over a high heat and throw in the carrots, sugarsnap peas and spring onions then stir-fry for 2–3 minutes. Add the cashews, garlic and ginger purée and cook for a further minute.

Sprinkle in the curry powder, Chinese five-spice and chilli flakes, then stir to create a dry mixture in the pan. Stir through the soy sauce.

Pour in the vegetable stock and mix in the cornflour. Keep the heat high, stirring frequently.

After 20 minutes, add the water chestnuts and peas, then cook for a further 10 minutes until thickened.

Remove from the heat and scatter with coriander before serving.

 **TAKE-OUT TIP**
Water chestnuts can be found conveniently canned in the world food aisle of large supermarkets, or at Chinese supermarkets.

✳

# CHOW MEIN

## SERVES 2 GENEROUSLY

**Chow mein is the king of noodle dishes, with slippery noodles, crunchy vegetables and a sweetly-spiced soy sauce. It's ready faster than it takes to get delivered from your local!**

300g (10oz) ready-to-wok soft noodles (ensure egg-free)
1 tbsp sunflower oil
2 tbsp cashew nuts
1 carrot, peeled and thinly sliced
6 sugarsnap peas, halved diagonally
6 small florets of broccoli, stalks trimmed
2 tsp ginger purée
2 garlic cloves, crushed
½ tsp Chinese five-spice
4 tbsp dark soy sauce
2 spring onions (scallions), finely chopped
small handful of coriander (cilantro) leaves, roughly torn
1 tbsp sesame seeds

✳

Place the noodles in a heatproof bowl and pour over enough hot water to cover. Allow them to stand for 4–5 minutes until they are easy to separate, then carefully drain away the hot water.

Heat the oil in a large wok over a high heat, then add the cashews, carrot, sugarsnap peas and broccoli. Stir-fry for 3–4 minutes until the vegetables are vibrant.

Stir in the ginger purée, garlic and Chinese five-spice and stir-fry for a further minute, then add the drained noodles and stir through the soy sauce. Stir-fry for 2 minutes.

Remove the wok from the heat. Stir through the spring onions and coriander, then sprinkle with the sesame seeds. Serve hot.

### TAKE-OUT TIP
Soaking the soft noodles for a few moments before cooking allows them to separate easily without breaking in the wok.

# CRISPY BEAN CURD AND BROCCOLI IN PLUM SAUCE

## SERVES 4

Sweet, sticky and oh-so-tasty, this restaurant classic has been given a fresh, vegan makeover. Serve with Extra fried rice (page 110) or some simple steamed greens.

**For the plum sauce**
6 ripe plums, stoned and roughly chopped
3 tbsp soft light brown sugar
2 tsp ginger purée
½ tsp dried chilli flakes
½ tsp Chinese five-spice
2 star anise
2 tbsp dark soy sauce

**For the bean curd and broccoli**
2 tbsp sunflower oil
2 tsp cornflour (cornstarch)
280g (9½oz) block of extra-firm tofu,
   drained and pressed (see page 14),
   then sliced into thin, even triangles
1 head of broccoli, broken into even florets
2 spring onions (scallions), finely sliced
small handful of coriander (cilantro) leaves,
   torn
1 tsp sesame seeds

✳

To make the plum sauce, put the plums and brown sugar into a large pan and place over a medium-high heat, then add the ginger purée, chilli flakes, Chinese five-spice and star anise. Simmer for 20 minutes, stirring frequently to avoid burning. After 20 minutes, add 100ml

(scant ½ cup) cold water, stir and simmer for a further 10 minutes. Remove from the heat, discard the star anise, then stir through the soy sauce. Use a stick blender to blitz the sauce until smooth and glossy.

Meanwhile, heat the oil in a large wok over a high heat. Scatter the cornflour onto a plate, then dip the tofu triangles into the cornflour, shaking off any excess.

Add the tofu triangles to the wok and cook for 4–5 minutes until golden and crisp, then turn over to cook the other side. Throw in the broccoli florets and stir-fry for a further 2–3 minutes until vibrant.

Pour the smooth plum sauce into the wok and stir-fry for 1 minute until the tofu and broccoli are coated. Remove from the heat and scatter over the spring onions, coriander and sesame seeds. Serve hot.

**GET AHEAD**
Tofu requires draining and pressing to give it a firmer texture. See page 14 for detailed instructions on how to do this.

# PINEAPPLE FRITTERS

## SERVES 4

**These Chinese favourites are quick to make, and even quicker to eat! Cinnamon-scented batter encases hot, sweet pineapple for an addictive taste that is the perfect end to your Chinese-style feast.**

400ml (1⅔ cups) sunflower oil, for frying
100g (scant 1 cup) self-raising flour
1 tsp sesame seeds
½ tsp ground cinnamon
200ml (generous ¾ cup) sparkling water
1 x 400g (14oz) can pineapple rings,
  drained of excess juice
1 tsp icing (confectioner's) sugar

✳

Begin to heat the oil in a large, heavy-based pan over a medium heat.

In a bowl, whisk together the flour, sesame seeds and cinnamon. Stir in the sparkling water and whisk to form a smooth batter.

Test if the oil is hot enough by dripping in a teaspoon of batter; if the batter rises and becomes golden, the oil is ready.

Dip the pineapple rings into the batter and shake off any excess. Carefully lower into the hot oil and fry for 4–5 minutes until golden, cooking 2 or 3 at a time to prevent the fritters from sticking to each other. Use a slotted spoon to remove the pineapple fritters from the pan and drain on kitchen paper.

Dust with a little icing sugar and serve hot.

✦ **TAKE-OUT TIP**

Canned pineapple rings are excellent in this recipe, however if you have fresh pineapple available the fritters will be extra delicious!

# WHITE CHOCOLATE MOUSSE AND KIWI

## SERVES 2

Create your own sweet dim sum dish to finish off your Chinese night in.
Dairy-free white chocolate can be found in the 'free from' sections of most
supermarkets, and adds rich sweetness to this dessert. Make sure that you use
silken tofu, as firm tofu will not create the desired bubbly mousse texture.

340g (12oz) silken tofu
100g (3½oz) dairy-free white chocolate,
  broken into even chunks
4 tbsp maple syrup
1 tsp good-quality vanilla extract
1 kiwi, peeled and thinly sliced into rounds

✳

Add the silken tofu to a high-powered
blender jug and blitz on high until smooth,
or use a stick blender to blitz the silken
tofu in a bowl.

Add the white chocolate pieces to a
heatproof bowl, then place over a pan of
simmering water, making sure the base of
the bowl does not touch the water. Stir
occasionally until the chocolate has melted
into a shiny liquid, then carefully pour into
the blended tofu.

Stir in the maple syrup and vanilla extract,
then blend again to ensure the mixture is
silky, smooth and fully combined.

Spoon into ramekin dishes, then cover and
refrigerate for at least 4 hours or overnight
until set.

Garnish each mousse with the kiwi slices
just before serving.

### GET AHEAD
The mousse requires some time to set
in the fridge, so it can be prepared a
day in advance; then all you have to do
before serving is slice the fresh kiwi.

# MIDDLE

## MENU FOR 2

Sometimes, only a vegan doner kebab will do. Don't let that stop you trying the other recipes in this chapter though, as Middle Eastern-style dishes are full of flavour, colour and satisfaction. Creating these fragrant classics at home is easier than you think, with minimal effort and maximum enjoyment.

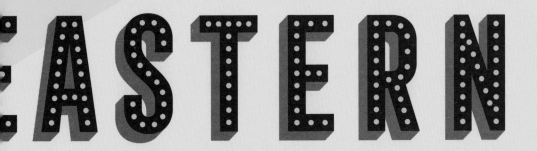

EASTERN

# STUFFED CHARD LEAVES

## SERVES 4 AS A SIDE DISH

**Stuffed vine leaves are a Middle Eastern delicacy, but let's face it, vine leaves are difficult to source and can be expensive. Enter the humble chard leaf as a wonderful substitute. I've also tried the recipe with spring green leaves and large kale leaves with excellent results; both are easy to source and great value for money.**

200g (7oz) basmati rice
handful of mint leaves, finely chopped
generous handful of dill, finely chopped
generous handful of flat-leaf parsley,
   finely chopped
handful of chives, finely chopped
juice of 1 unwaxed lemon
drizzle of extra virgin olive oil
generous pinch of sea salt
10 large chard leaves, halved lengthways,
   tough lower stems removed
sesame seeds, for sprinkling

✳

Add the basmati rice to a pan and cover with 400ml (1⅔ cups) boiling water. Simmer for 12–15 minutes until tender. Meanwhile, preheat the oven to 180°C/350°F/gas mark 4.

Carefully spoon the rice into a large bowl and stir through the chopped herbs. Stir in the lemon juice and olive oil until combined with the rice and herbs. Season to taste with the sea salt.

Lay out one chard leaf half in front of you. Spoon 1 tablespoon of the herbed rice into the centre of the leaf, then fold the long sides inwards to meet in the centre. Then start rolling neatly from a short side until you form a sealed parcel. Place the stuffed leaf in a baking tray and repeat until you've used all of the leaves. Pack the stuffed leaves tightly next to each other in the baking tray and pour in 200ml (generous ¾ cup) boiling water. Cover loosely with foil, then bake in the oven for 30 minutes.

Carefully remove from the oven and allow to stand for a few minutes before sprinkling with sesame seeds and serving.

### GET AHEAD

✳
    These stuffed chard leaves can be
    served hot or cold. They will keep for
◦   up to 2 days in the fridge, and make
    a great side dish or snack at any time
    of day.

# POMEGRANATE TABBOULEH

## SERVES 4 AS A SIDE DISH

**This traditional herb salad makes a refreshing side dish to my Carrot, date and chickpea tagine (page 137). Ready in just 15 minutes, tabbouleh will become your Middle Eastern fast food staple.**

80g (3oz) bulgar wheat
handful of flat-leaf parsley, finely chopped
handful of mint leaves, finely chopped
seeds from 1 pomegranate
generous drizzle of extra virgin olive oil
juice of 1 unwaxed lemon
generous pinch of sea salt

✳

Add the bulgar wheat to a large, heatproof bowl and pour over enough boiling water to just cover it. Cover with a plate or cling film (plastic wrap) and leave to stand for 10 minutes until the water has fully absorbed.

Separate the bulgar wheat with a fork and stir in the parsley, mint and pomegranate seeds.

Drizzle over the olive oil and lemon juice, then stir to mix through. Season to taste with sea salt.

### GET AHEAD
No time to gather seeds from a pomegranate? You can buy prepared pomegranate seeds from most supermarkets.

# BABA GANOUSH

### SERVES 2 AS A DIP

This is the perfect Saturday afternoon recipe – simply throw a few ingredients into a slow cooker, then blitz with olive oil, lemon juice and parsley for a Middle Eastern-inspired dip ready for your Saturday-night feast. The beady-eyed among you will notice the non-traditional addition of smooth peanut butter in place of sesame tahini; it gives a richer, smokier flavour, but feel free to switch back to tahini if you prefer to keep it authentic. Serve alongside hummus, olives and flatbreads for a delicious meze.

1 large aubergine (eggplant), diced into even 3cm (1¼in) chunks
2 tbsp smooth peanut butter
1 garlic clove, crushed
generous drizzle of extra virgin olive oil, plus extra to serve
juice of ¼ unwaxed lemon
small handful of flat-leaf parsley, finely chopped
generous pinch of smoked sea salt
generous pinch of smoked paprika

✳

Preheat the slow cooker by setting it to low.

Add the aubergine, peanut butter and garlic to the slow cooker, stir, then place the lid over. Cook on low for 4 hours until the aubergine is tender.

Spoon the softened aubergine, garlic and peanut butter into a food processor or high-powered jug blender, then pour in the olive oil and lemon juice. Blitz until semi-smooth.

Scoop the purée into a bowl and fold through most of the flat-leaf parsley. Season to taste with smoked sea salt. Spoon into a serving bowl, drizzle with olive oil and sprinkle over the smoked paprika and remaining parsley. Serve warm, or refrigerate once the dip has cooled.

 **GET AHEAD**
If you're blitzing the dip in a food processor or blender, there's no need to remove the aubergine (eggplant) skin. If you'd prefer to purée the cooked aubergine by hand using a potato masher, then simply peel off the skin before dicing. Use a good-quality vegetable peeler to do this for ease and to save time.

# GREEK SALAD

## SERVES 4 AS A SIDE DISH

Did you know that little bag of soggy salad you often get from your local is one of the most wasted food items? It's no surprise as the salad usually gets delivered soggy, browning and limp, bearing little resemblance to its fresh counterpart. This Greek salad is fresh, crisp and full of herbs, with a zing of lemon juice that makes it a refreshing side to any take-out dish.

300g (10oz) cherry tomatoes, sliced
  in a variety of ways (see tip)
¼ cucumber, sliced into half-moon shapes
10 pitted black olives, halved
½ small red onion, thinly sliced
juice of ½ unwaxed lemon
2 tbsp extra virgin olive oil
small handful of dill, finely chopped
small handful of flat-leaf parsley, finely
  chopped
2 tsp flaked (slivered) almonds
sea salt and black pepper

✳

Add the tomatoes, cucumber, olives and onion to a large bowl.

Stir through the lemon juice, olive oil, dill and parsley.

Scatter with the flaked almonds and gently stir through. Season to taste with sea salt and black pepper.

### TAKE-OUT TIP
Go rogue with your tomato preparation! Quarter a few, slice some into rings, halve a handful and dice a couple. This all adds texture to the salad, and also means that you don't have to spend time with technical and specific chopping.

# CARROT, DATE AND CHICKPEA TAGINE

### SERVES 4 GENEROUSLY

**Don't wait to enjoy fragrant tagine at your local Lebanese restaurant, create an authentic-tasting classic in the comfort of your home. Let the oven do all of the hard work – and there's no need for a specialist tagine pot either; a lidded casserole dish will get the job done!**

**Suitable for freezing**

1 tbsp sunflower oil
3 carrots, peeled and roughly chopped into 3cm (1¼in) pieces
2 medium sweet potatoes, peeled and roughly chopped into 3cm (1¼in) pieces
2 red onions, peeled and quartered
2 garlic cloves, thinly sliced
2 tsp harissa paste
2 tsp ground cumin
1 tsp ground turmeric
1 tsp ginger purée
1 x 400g (14oz) can chickpeas, drained and thoroughly rinsed
10 dates, pitted
juice of ½ unwaxed lemon
sea salt and black pepper
handful of flat-leaf parsley, roughly chopped

✳

Preheat the oven to 180°C/350°F/gas mark 4.

Heat the oil in a lidded hob-to-oven casserole dish, add the carrots, sweet potatoes and red onions and stir on the hob over a high heat for 4–5 minutes until the vegetables begin to soften.

Stir in the garlic, harissa paste, cumin, turmeric and ginger purée, then stir in the chickpeas and dates, followed by 100ml (scant ½ cup) cold water.

Place the lid over the dish, then transfer to the oven for 45 minutes until the vegetables are tender and the cooking liquid is simmering.

Carefully remove the dish from the oven and squeeze over the lemon juice. Season generously with salt and pepper, then sprinkle over the parsley just before serving.

**TAKE-OUT TIP**
If you don't have time to shop for dates, dried apricots or large, juicy sultanas (golden raisins) from your store cupboard make a great alternative.

# GREEK LENTIL
# MOUSSAKA

## SERVES 4

Demystify the preparation and cooking of your favourite Greek dish: moussaka. Perfect layers of aubergine (eggplant) and cinnamon-infused lentil 'mince' make a deliciously satisfying main meal. Serve with crusty bread and a green salad.

**Suitable for freezing**

1 tbsp sunflower oil
1 onion, diced
1 garlic clove, crushed
1 tsp ground cinnamon
1 tsp ground paprika
1 tsp dried oregano
1 tsp dried mixed herbs
1 x 400g (14oz) can chopped tomatoes
1 x 400g (14oz) can green lentils, drained
   and thoroughly rinsed
sea salt and black pepper
2 aubergines (eggplants), thinly sliced
   into rounds
small handful of parsley, roughly chopped

**For the white sauce**
1 tbsp sunflower oil
1 tbsp plain (all-purpose) flour
250ml (1 cup) unsweetened soya milk

✳

Preheat the oven to 200°C/400°F/gas mark 6. Heat the oil in a large pan, add the onion and cook for 2–3 minutes until it begins to soften. Add the garlic, cinnamon, paprika, oregano and mixed herbs then cook for another minute. Pour in the tomatoes and lentils, then simmer for 10 minutes, stirring occasionally. Season generously.

Arrange a layer of aubergine in the base of an ovenproof dish, then spoon over a layer of the lentil mince. Continue with layers of aubergine slices and lentil mince until there is 2cm (¾in) left at the top of the dish. Bake in the oven for 15 minutes.

Meanwhile, prepare the white sauce. Add the oil and flour to a pan over a low heat, then use a small balloon whisk to form a roux. When the two ingredients have formed a paste, pour in half the soya milk and whisk continuously until it begins to thicken. Add the remaining soya milk and whisk again until thickened. Season to taste.

Carefully remove the moussaka from the oven and pour over the white sauce. Return the dish to the oven for 45 minutes until the sauce is bubbling and golden at the edges. Remove from the oven and serve hot with the parsley scattered on top.

✦ **GET AHEAD**

The lentil mince can be prepared up to 3 days in advance when kept in the fridge, or frozen and fully defrosted before use in this moussaka.

# APRICOT, PISTACHIO AND CHICKPEA KOFTE

## SERVES 2

These flavoursome kofte are little bites of heaven, served in warmed flatbreads with a lemon and black pepper tahini sauce. Baked instead of fried, for all the flavour without the extra fats. Add cucumber and crisp salad leaves to your flatbreads for extra crunch.

**The kofte are suitable for freezing**

**For the kofte**
1 tbsp sunflower oil
1 onion, diced
1 tsp ground cumin
½ tsp dried oregano
1 tbsp shelled pistachios
1 x 400g (14oz) can chickpeas, thoroughly
    drained and rinsed
1 tbsp brown sauce
140g (5oz) dried apricots, finely chopped
sea salt

**To serve**
2 tbsp tahini
juice of ¼ unwaxed lemon
pinch of black pepper
4 small flatbreads (ensure dairy-free),
    warmed
small handful of flat-leaf parsley leaves,
    torn

✳

Preheat the oven to 180°C/350°F/gas mark 4. Heat the oil and onion in a pan over a medium-high heat for 2–3 minutes until the onion begins to soften. Stir in the cumin, oregano and pistachios and cook for a further 2 minutes.

In the meantime, add the chickpeas to a bowl and pour over enough boiling water to cover. Leave for 5 minutes, then drain.

Add the cooked onion and pistachio mixture to a blender or food processor, along with any remaining oil from the pan. Add the drained chickpeas and brown sauce and a generous pinch of sea salt, then blitz to form a thick, semi-smooth paste. Stir through the dried apricots. Scoop out walnut-sized amounts of the mixture and roll into approximately 8 balls. Place on a baking sheet and bake in the oven for 25–30 minutes until golden.

Meanwhile, mix together the tahini and lemon juice until combined. Season to taste with black pepper.

Remove the cooked kofte from the oven, load into the flatbreads and spoon over the tahini sauce. Scatter with parsley and serve.

✦ **GET AHEAD**
✳   Soaking canned chickpeas in hot water allows them to blend more easily.
∘   Cooked chickpeas sold in glass jars are often softer, therefore this step can be omitted if using the jarred variety.

# ONE-POT HARISSA BAKED FALAFEL

## SERVES 4

**Shop-bought falafel are convenient, but rarely live up to the hot-from-the-fryer version. This 30-minute recipe elevates ready-to-eat falafel and delivers delicious Middle Eastern flavours – all in one pot. Load into toasted pitta breads, or use them to dip into the spiced sauce – the choice is yours.**

1 x 400g (14oz) can chopped tomatoes
2 tsp harissa paste
1 small red onion, thinly sliced into rings
12 pitted green olives
8 ready-to-eat falafel (ensure vegan)
handful of flat-leaf parsley, finely chopped
generous pinch of sea salt
1 tbsp unsweetened soya yogurt
4 pitta breads, toasted

✳

Preheat the oven to 200°C/400°F/gas mark 6.

Put the chopped tomatoes into a lidded ovenproof dish and stir through the harissa paste. Stir in the red onion and olives.

Place the falafel in the tomato mix, ensuring the top half of each one is visible. This will allow them to brown and crisp gently.

Place the lid on the dish, then bake in the oven for 30 minutes until the sauce is bubbling and the falafel are golden.

Carefully remove the lid and scatter over the parsley and sea salt. Spoon over the soya yogurt and serve hot with toasted pitta breads.

 **TAKE-OUT TIP**
Ready-to-eat falafel are available in the deli aisles at most supermarkets, but do ensure they are egg- and dairy-free.

# PITTA SAMBUSAK WITH PISTACHIOS AND POTATOES

## SERVES 4

These baked pitta pockets have all of the flavour of Lebanese sambusak, without the need to make a tricky pastry, or any deep-frying. They are also a great way to use up any pitta breads, potatoes and onions that have been lurking in the kitchen all week! Serve with vibrant Pink pickles (opposite).

3 tbsp sunflower oil
2 baking potatoes, scrubbed clean and cut
  into 2cm (¾in) cubes
2 onions, sliced
6 closed-cup mushrooms, brushed clean
  and diced
pinch of ground cinnamon
pinch of ground cumin
handful of shelled pistachios, roughly
  chopped
4 pitta breads, halved
1 tbsp sesame seeds
sea salt and black pepper

✳

Preheat the oven to 200°C/400°F/gas mark 6.

Add 2 tablespoons of the sunflower oil to a large frying pan (skillet) and place over a medium-high heat. Throw in the potatoes, onions and mushrooms and cook for 10–12 minutes until the potatoes have browned and become softened, and the onions are caramelized.

Stir in the cinnamon, cumin and pistachios and cook for 2 minutes, stirring frequently. Season generously with salt and pepper.

Gently open the pitta bread halves by scoring a sharp knife through the opening, so they can be filled. Add up to 2 tablespoons of the potato filling to each pitta pocket, then place on baking trays. Brush the tops of the pittas with the remaining oil, then sprinkle over the sesame seeds.

Bake in the oven for 10–15 minutes until the edges are crisp and the sesame seeds are golden.

 **GET AHEAD**
The pistachio and potato filling can be cooked up to 2 days in advance and then kept in the fridge in a sealed container. Simply load into your pittas before baking in the oven.

# PINK
# PICKLES

### SERVES 4 AS A RELISH

**If you've ever looked longingly at those pink-hued pickles in your falafel flatbread wrap and wondered just what they are – it's likely that you're feasting on pickled turnip, that has been combined with beetroot (beet) to give it that rosy tone. Pickling turnips can take at least a week (who has the time for that!), but this recipe is ready in three simple steps, and reassuringly takes just a couple of hours. Spoon over Carrot, date and chickpea tagine (page 137) for contrasting colour and a pickled zing, or serve with Pitta sambusak with pistachios and potatoes (opposite) for addictive crunch.**

2 red onions, thinly sliced
½ small red cabbage, thinly sliced
4 radishes, quartered
100ml (scant ½ cup) apple cider vinegar
1 tbsp maple syrup
pinch of dried chilli flakes
finely grated zest of 1 unwaxed lemon

✳

Put the red onions into a heatproof bowl and pour over enough boiling water to cover them. Allow to stand for 10 minutes, then carefully drain away the hot water.

Add the cabbage, radishes, cider vinegar, maple syrup, chilli flakes and lemon zest to the bowl and stir.

Cover with cling film (plastic wrap) or a plate, and allow to pickle for at least 2 hours.

 **GET AHEAD**

These pickles are ready to enjoy after just 2 hours of pickling, but they can be transferred to a clean jar and refrigerated once fully cooled. Refrigerate for up to 2 weeks to enjoy the best crunch and flavour.

# JACKFRUIT DONER KEBAB

## SERVES 4

When the need arises for a Saturday-night kebab, you can step away from that greasy shop and create your own in no time. Packed with all the smoky flavour you'd expect, but with a sweet, caramelized onion edge, you'll be hooked from the first bite.

**The cooked jackfruit is suitable for freezing**

1 tbsp sunflower oil
1 onion, thinly sliced
1 tsp soft light brown sugar
1 garlic clove, crushed
1 tsp smoked paprika
pinch of ground cumin
pinch of ground cinnamon
1 x 400g (14oz) can jackfruit, drained and rinsed, then broken into strands
juice of ¼ unwaxed lemon
handful of flat-leaf parsley, finely chopped
sea salt

**To serve**
4 pitta breads, toasted
4 tsp vegan mayonnaise
pink pickles (see page 145)
handful of chopped iceberg lettuce
¼ cucumber, sliced
small handful of dill, leaves picked

Heat the oil and onion in a frying pan (skillet) over a medium-high heat for 5 minutes, stirring occasionally to prevent sticking. Sprinkle in the brown sugar and cook for a further 5 minutes until lightly browned and caramelized.

Stir in the garlic, paprika, cumin and cinnamon and cook for a further minute.

Add the jackfruit and stir to coat in the spices and onion. Cook for 10 minutes, stirring frequently to avoid sticking.

Remove the pan from the heat and stir in the lemon juice and parsley. Season to taste with a generous pinch of sea salt.

Load the cooked jackfruit into toasted pitta breads with mayonnaise, pink pickles, iceburg lettuce, cucumber slices and dill.

 **TAKE-OUT TIP**
To give jackfruit the perfect 'pulled' texture, simply use your hands to easily tear the chunks into strands.

# AUBERGINE AND ORZO GUVEC

## SERVES 4

*This twist on the classic Turkish casserole is named after the dish it is cooked in, guvec. If you don't have a guvec to cook in, simply use a casserole dish or lidded pan. Serve in bowls with crusty bread to dip, for a taste of the Middle East.*

**Suitable for freezing**

1 tbsp sunflower oil
1 aubergine (eggplant), roughly chopped
   into 2cm (¾in) chunks
1 red onion, roughly chopped
1 courgette (zucchini), roughly chopped
   into 2cm (¾in) chunks
1 tsp dried oregano
½ tsp ground cinnamon
1 x 400g (14oz) can chopped tomatoes
1 tsp harissa paste
10 cherry tomatoes
10 pitted green olives
4 tbsp dried orzo (ensure egg-free)
1 tbsp pine nuts, lightly toasted
small handful of flat-leaf parsley
sea salt

✳

Heat the oil in a large lidded pan or hob-proof casserole dish, add the aubergine, then begin to brown over a medium-high heat for 4–5 minutes.

Add the red onion, courgette, oregano and cinnamon, then cook for a further 2 minutes, stirring frequently to prevent burning.

Pour in the chopped tomatoes and harissa, then stir through the cherry tomatoes and olives. Loosely place the lid on the dish, reduce the heat to low-medium and simmer for 15 minutes, stirring occasionally.

Stir in the orzo and simmer for 10 minutes. Remove from the heat, scatter over the pine nuts and flat-leaf parsley and season to taste with a pinch of sea salt.

   **TAKE-OUT TIP**
   Orzo is a rice-shaped pasta, which is
   available in large supermarkets – just
   make sure that it is egg-free.

# DATE, NUTMEG AND ORANGE PASTRIES

**MAKES 8**

Whether it's an after-dinner treat or a sweet snack with a cup of tea, these sticky pastries are fragrant and satisfying, as well as being simple and quick to bake. Many brands of shop-bought puff pastry are accidentally vegan, as vegetable oil is used instead of dairy butter, meaning you can create these pastries with minimal effort.

250g (9oz) dates, pitted and roughly chopped
½ tsp grated nutmeg
finely grated zest and juice of 1 unwaxed orange
1 sheet of ready-rolled puff pastry (ensure dairy-free)

✳

Add the chopped dates, nutmeg and orange zest to a bowl and pour over the orange juice. Allow to infuse for 10–15 minutes.

Preheat the oven to 200°C/400°F/gas mark 6 and line a baking sheet with baking parchment. Lay out the pastry sheet on a chopping board.

Drain any excess juice from the soaked date mix. Spoon the mix onto the pastry sheet, spreading it evenly to the edges and corners.

Starting from one short end, roll the pastry inwards, tightly and evenly to form a long roll. Then use a sharp knife to slice the roll into 8 even rounds.

Place the rounds on the lined baking sheet and bake for 10–12 minutes until golden. Allow to cool a little before removing from the tray.

 **GET AHEAD**
Pre-chopped dates can be found in supermarkets (usually with the baking ingredients) which will save you pitting and chopping time and effort!

# LOKMA CHURROS

Lokma is delicious, syrup-coated, fried dough, here made even better by fusing it with Mediterranean churros. Dip these in cinnamon-sprinkled maple syrup, for a sweet, smoky treat.

**For the lokma churros**
2 tbsp sunflower oil, plus 800ml
    (3½ cups) sunflower oil for frying
3 tbsp caster (superfine) sugar
½ tsp sea salt
½ tsp ground cinnamon
130g (1 cup) plain (all-purpose) flour

**For the cinnamon-maple dip**
4 tbsp maple syrup
pinch of ground cinnamon
small piece of dark chocolate
    (ensure dairy-free), grated

✳

Put the 2 tablespoons of oil, sugar, salt and cinnamon into a pan, then pour in 250ml (1 cup) cold water. Bring to a simmer over a medium heat, then stir in the flour and mix until a firm ball of dough is created.

Heat the oil for frying in a deep fryer or deep, heavy-based pan – test that the oil is hot enough by dropping in a small piece of the dough. It should become golden and rise to the surface within 1 minute.

Fit a piping bag with a star-shaped nozzle and fill the bag with the dough. Squeeze 5cm (2in) long pieces of the dough into the hot oil, using scissors to cut the dough from the nozzle. Cook for 2–3 minutes until golden, then carefully remove from the oil and drain on kitchen paper or a clean tea towel.

In a bowl, stir together the maple syrup and cinnamon. Quickly toss the cooked lokma churros in the syrup then place on a serving plate. Scatter over the grated chocolate and serve while the churros are warm.

**GET AHEAD**
The dough can be make a day in advance and kept refrigerated, then brought to room temperature before piping.

# INDEX